CLEANSING

YOUR HOME

FROM EVIL

CLEANSING

KICK THE DEVIL OUT

YOUR HOME

OF YOUR HOUSE

FROM EVIL

JENNIFER LECLAIRE

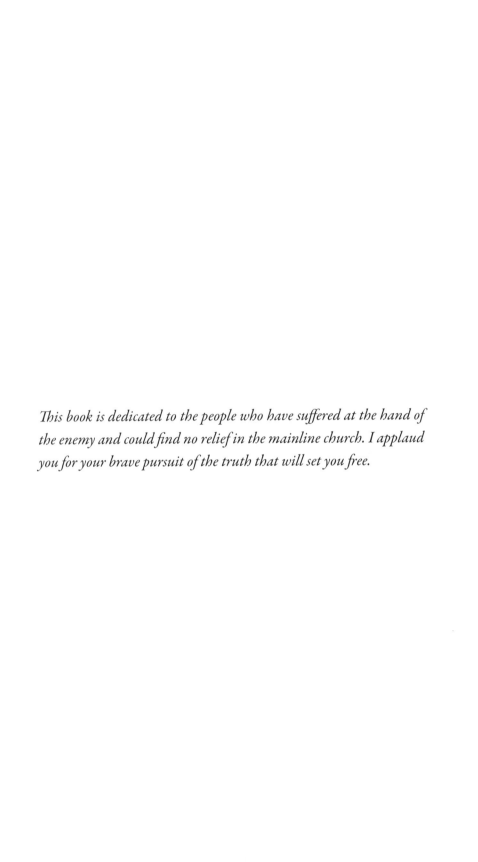

This book is dedicated to the people who have suffered at the hand of the enemy and could find no relief in the mainline church. I applaud you for your brave pursuit of the truth that will set you free.

ACKNOWLEDGMENTS

As always, I want to thank my dear friend Larry Sparks for being bold and brave enough to tackle somewhat controversial topics that, when presented in the light of Scripture, set people free. I am grateful for my Awakening Prayer Hubs leaders around the world who have my back in prayer. I am thankful for my church family at Awakening House of Prayer who helps keep me sharp and on the cutting edge to dig out revelation in the Word that brings healing and deliverance to the Body of Christ.

DESTINY IMAGE® PUBLISHERS, INC.
P.O. Box 310, Shippensburg, PA 17257-0310
"Promoting Inspired Lives."

This book and all other Destiny Image and Destiny Image Fiction books are available at Christian bookstores and distributors worldwide.

Cover design by Eileen Rockwell.

For more information on foreign distributors, call 717-532-3040.
Reach us on the Internet: www.destinyimage.com.

ISBN 13 TP: 978-0-7684-5882-4

ISBN 13 eBook: 978-0-7684-5883-1

ISBN 13 HC: 978-0-7684-5885-5

ISBN 13 LP: 978-0-7684-5884-8

For Worldwide Distribution, Printed in the U.S.A.

1 2 3 4 5 6 7 8 / 25 24 23 22 21

CONTENTS

CHAPTER 1

ARE DEMONS
HIDING IN YOUR HOME?

H aunted houses are a popular Hollywood storyline that sends adrenaline pumping through the veins of viewers in dark theaters around the world. From William Castle's *13 Ghosts* in the 1960s, to Tim Burton's *Beetlejuice* in 1988, to the more comical *Ghostbusters* in 1984, the dark side of the supernatural has earned Hollywood filmmakers millions upon millions of dollars—and demonstrated some fact and fiction about demonology along the way.

Hollywood calls it paranormal activity. Discerning Christians call it demons hiding—even lurking—in the closets, attics, and even displayed openly on bookshelves and media cabinets in our homes. Yes, there could be demons crouching behind veils of darkness in your house. They may not be moving furniture around or talking to you through your television set à la Steven Spielberg's *Poltergeist*, but make no mistake—these unseen trespassers are on a mission to steal, kill, and destroy your life (see John 10:10). Yes, there may be a boogie man under your bed, for real!

What are demons? Evil spirits, technically fallen angels. Once upon a time, lucifer was a beautiful angel, but in his pride he determined to be like the God who created him. He launched an insurrection in heaven, convincing one-third of the heavenly host to follow his perverted leadership. You might say it this way: God had a lot of demons in His house and had to cleanse His heavenly home from evil. It's important to understand demons are always looking for homes, and if they tried to inhabit heaven, they won't hesitate to inhabit your abode.

SATAN WAS ONCE BEAUTIFUL

Remember, lucifer was once the most beautiful angel in heaven. In Ezekiel 28:12-15, we read God Himself sharing about the splendor of His creation, lucifer, as well as his demise:

> You were the seal of perfection, full of wisdom and perfect in beauty. You were in Eden, the garden of God; every precious stone was your covering: the sardius, topaz, and diamond, beryl, onyx, and jasper, sapphire, turquoise, and emerald with gold. The workmanship of your timbrels and pipes was prepared for you on the day you were created.
>
> You were the anointed cherub who covers; I established you; you were on the holy mountain of God; you walked back and forth in the midst of fiery stones. You were perfect in your ways from the day you were created, till iniquity was found in you.

Lucifer was anointed. He was beautiful. That's important to note because he still operates as an angel of light today (see 2 Cor. 11:14). In other words, some believers have demons in their homes attached to an outwardly beautiful object. Just because a piece of art or sculpture or jewelry is visually appealing doesn't mean it's not carrying demon powers. That's part of the deception we want to break in the pages of this book.

In Isaiah 14:12-15, we see the fall of lucifer:

> *How you are fallen from heaven, O Lucifer, son of the morning! How you are cut down to the ground, you who weakened the nations! For you have said in your heart: "I will ascend into heaven, I will exalt my throne above the stars of God; I will also sit on the mount of the congregation on the farthest sides of the north; I will ascend above the heights of the clouds, I will be like the Most High." Yet you shall be brought down to Sheol, to the lowest depths of the Pit.*

Lucifer fell from heaven because of pride and selfish ambition. Notice how the Lord says he wakened the nations. The enemy has real power in the earth. As a matter of fact, Jesus Himself called satan the prince of this world (see John 14:30). Some translations call him the ruler of the world. Some believers don't understand how satan can be the ruler of the world if God created the world and all that is in it. Here's how. Jesus said:

> *When an unclean spirit goes out of a man, he goes through dry places, seeking rest, and finds none. Then he says, "I will return to my house from which I came." And when he comes, he finds it empty, swept, and put in order. Then he goes and takes with*

him seven other spirits more wicked than himself, and they enter and dwell there; and the last state of that man is worse than the first (Matthew 12:43-45).

THE SNAKE IN THE GARDEN

Remember, God cast lucifer and the other hundreds of thousands of fallen angels out of His presence—out of His heavenly house. Revelation 12:7-9 recalls:

And war broke out in heaven: Michael and his angels fought with the dragon; and the dragon and his angels fought, but they did not prevail, nor was a place found for them in heaven any longer. So the great dragon was cast out, that serpent of old, called the Devil and Satan, who deceives the whole world; he was cast to the earth, and his angels were cast out with him.

Now let's refer back to Christ's words in Matthew 12 above. Although Jesus was talking about a person receiving deliverance, the same principle holds true for a house. Satan could not get back into heaven after God cast him out, but satan found the next best thing to the garden of God in heaven—the garden of God in the earth, also known as the Genesis 2 Garden of Eden.

Genesis 2:8 tells us God planted a garden eastward in Eden and He put the first man, Adam, in the garden. Every tree with edible fruit grew in the garden, and the Tree of Life was in the middle of the garden, next to the Tree of the Knowledge of Good and Evil. A river watered the garden. God told Adam he could eat of any tree in the garden, except of the Tree of the Knowledge of Good and Evil. Later, He took a rib out of Adam's side and created Eve. Soon enough, the devil tried to get in Adam's house.

Now the serpent was more cunning than any beast of the field which the Lord God had made. And he said to the woman, "Has God indeed said, 'You shall not eat of every tree of the garden'?" And the woman said to the serpent, "We may eat the fruit of the trees of the garden; but of the fruit of the tree which is in the midst of the garden, God has said, 'You shall not eat it, nor shall you touch it, lest you die.'"

Then the serpent said to the woman, "You will not surely die. For God knows that in the day you eat of it your eyes will be opened, and you will be like God, knowing good and evil."

So when the woman saw that the tree was good for food, that it was pleasant to the eyes, and a tree desirable to make one wise, she took of its fruit and ate. She also gave to her husband with her, and he ate. Then the eyes of both of them were opened, and they knew that they were naked; and they sewed fig leaves together and made themselves coverings (Genesis 3:1-7).

EATING DECEPTIVE FRUIT

Let's review this: God told Adam not to eat of the fruit of the Tree of Knowledge of Good and Evil. He disobeyed God. The fruit seemed appealing—it was pleasant to the eyes. Again, we can bring things into our home that are pleasant to our eyes but evil to the core. The fruit was good for wisdom. We can bring books and media into our home in the name of self-help that carry demonic influences.

You might say, "Well, the tree was already in Adam's home." Technically, the tree was in the world and Adam's home was in the world. I sometimes wonder what would have happened if Adam had been more spiritually curious and instead of just resisting the temptation to eat the fruit of the Knowledge of the Tree of Good and Evil, he asked God to remove it. Would God have uprooted the tree? Or was Adam supposed to chop it down? If Adam had inquired of the Lord about the dangers of the forbidden fruit, would he have fallen for the enemy's trap? If he knew the consequences, would he have entered the temptation?

What's more, First Timothy 2:14 tells us, "And Adam was not deceived, but the woman being deceived, fell into transgression." We'll talk more about this later, but the reality is someone else can bring cursed objects into your house and it can affect your life, too. And you are deceived if you don't think it will. We don't have immunity against what we tolerate. If your teenager is listening to demonic music and you don't shut it down, you're opening a demonic portal in your home.

The enemy doesn't fight fair and he's ravenous. That's why Peter warned in First Peter 5:8-9:

> Be well balanced (temperate, sober of mind), be vigilant and cautious at all times; for that enemy of yours, the devil, roams around like a lion roaring [in fierce hunger], seeking someone to seize upon and devour. Withstand him; be firm in faith [against his onset—rooted, established, strong, immovable, and determined], knowing that the same (identical) sufferings

are appointed to your brotherhood (the whole body of Christians) throughout the world (AMPC).

DEMONS IN MY DRAWER

Before I relocated from my beach condo to my downtown Ft. Lauderdale loft in 2017, I threw away—or donated when appropriate—bags upon bags of clothing and other items I had accumulated over 10 years and no longer needed. I knew I didn't have any evil objects in my home, but I wanted to make a clean start in the new loft. (And who wants to move a bunch of stuff you never use, right?)

The loft was swept clean but it wasn't empty when I moved in. Since lofts by nature are oversized with 24-foot ceilings and wide open spaces, I knew I would need to invest in new furniture and wall art. Traveling the world monthly, I also knew I would probably not have time to do that, so instead I negotiated to buy most of the furniture—including a 15-foot couch and other oversized items—because it looked great right where it was.

Before I settled in, I looked through every kitchen drawer and the cupboards, and there was nothing unusual left behind. I did what I thought was a clean sweep, including cleansing prayers. Nevertheless, the first few nights in the loft I had a hard time sleeping. I was up and down all night long. I felt like I was on high alert. After several days of this, I was exhausted. I reasoned whether my restlessness was because of the downtown sounds rather than the beach sounds. No. I reasoned whether

I was out of sorts because it was a new place. No, I sleep in hotels all over the world just fine.

Then one morning as I set out to do my 6 a.m. *Mornings with the Holy Spirit* prophetic prayer broadcast on Facebook, I needed a pen to write down a sudden revelation. I hadn't yet unpacked every box and was trying to figure out where to find a pen in a hurry. That's when I noticed something I hadn't seen before. There were two thin drawers on a desk near the front door. They were almost hidden from sight. I figured, "There must be pen in the drawer on this desk." When I opened the drawer, I found more than a pen. I found demons.

In the drawer, I found Jezebelic comic books. The sight of the covers staring me in the face literally shocked me. I gasped. One of the comic books was called *The Wicked and the Divine*. It had on the cover a woman with her face painted, like Jezebel in the Bible before Jehu rode up to the wicked queen sitting in a window ready for war (see 2 Kings 9:30). Another comic in the same series had the Jezebelic woman pictured with a cross-laden necklace and what looked like Zodiac symbols on her bracelet. When I destroyed the comic books, I slept better than a baby from that point on.

Jezebel is representative of a spirit. I write about this in my book *The Spiritual Warrior's Guide to Defeating Jezebel* and teach about it in *Will the Real Jezebel Please Stand Up?* on schoolofthespirit.tv. Jezebel is a seducing principality that releases a power called witchcraft. Witchcraft is the power of the enemy just as the Holy Spirit is the power of God. When witchcraft attacks, it can cause exhaustion, sickness, and all manner of evil fruit. The reason I could not sleep was because these

Jezebelic comic books were in my home and my spirit was on high alert to the danger lurking in my drawer until I found them.

My story just goes to show, you never know what's in your house from a previous occupant. Demons had a right of entry through a former occupant. This is why when the Israelites were taking territory in the Promised Land, the Lord wanted them to not only drive out the inhabitants but also their idols—and not marry foreign wives. Although the people who sold me the condo had moved out, I had to dispossess the occupying demons.

After I dealt with those demons, I haven't had any trouble. (By the way, this is why you should also look in drawers of hotel rooms you stay in. A certain chain has a false testament of Jesus in the nightstand that must be removed from your room before you go to sleep. And people do wicked things in hotel rooms. You need to check the drawers and pray to cleanse the room when you get there.)

THE CURSE OF INFIRMITY AND DIVORCE

Years before my loft incident, a close friend of mine had strange noises and happenings in her home. Fans would turn themselves on. Rattling noises persisted. Sometimes in the spirit she would see demons above the bed in the master bedroom.

Being savvy to spiritual house cleansing, she and her husband had completed several sweeps through their house, but serious problems were persisting. After hearing her story, I realized there were still demons hiding somewhere. It seemed there was actually a curse on the home itself.

Upon investigating, neighbors reported something especially troublesome—every couple who had previously lived in the home was divorced. You might not find that altogether unusual with high divorce rates common, but when we dug deeper we discovered one person who lived there turned up with severe mental illness. Physical illness was prevalent among those who took up residence in the house. Beyond that, the security alarm went off frequently for no reason. The dog would bark just before the alarm went off. It was an unseen enemy lurking through the home.

During the late-night hours, my friends sometimes heard doors slamming, pipes rattling, and other strange phenomena that made them sure the house was haunted with evil spirits. Others whose homes have been demonized have reported pictures moving, hearing footsteps walking, or feeling a chilling wind blowing through the house even when the windows are closed. Others report smelling stench and they can't figure out where it's coming from.

Distressing spirits in your house can cause you to act out of sorts. Evil spirits in your home can torment you in your sleep and whisper vain imaginations to your soul while you are awake. We see this reality in the story of King Saul. First Samuel 18:10-11 reads:

> *And it happened on the next day that the distressing spirit from God came upon Saul, and he prophesied inside the house. So David played music with his hand, as at other times; but there was a spear in Saul's hand. And Saul cast the spear, for he said, "I will pin David to the wall!" But David escaped his presence twice.*

IT'S NOT ALL LIKE POLTERGEIST

Despite what we've seen in Hollywood's haunted house and paranormal movies, sometimes it's not so easy to detect evil spirits in your home. The most strategic demons don't want to be found. They hide from view. They count on you not knowing they are there. Paul the apostle warned us not be clueless about how the enemy operates: "We're not oblivious to his sly ways!" (2 Cor. 2:11 MSG).

Let me put it another way. Not every home demons inhabit has obviously outward manifestations of evil. As much as Hollywood exploits the paranormal, the dark side is not always so dramatic. We need to understand sinful activities and cursed objects can wreak havoc in our lives in more ways than one. The presence of demons in your home can breed strife in your marriage, sickness in your body, financial distress, and more.

The good news is you have authority in your home. Jesus told His disciples:

> *I saw Satan falling like a lightning [flash] from heaven. Behold! I have given you authority and power to trample upon serpents and scorpions, and [physical and mental strength and ability] over all the power that the enemy [possesses]; and nothing shall in any way harm you* (Luke 10:18-19 AMPC).

The Passion Translation puts it this way:

> *Now you understand that I have imparted to you my authority to trample over his kingdom. You will trample upon every*

demon before you and overcome every power Satan possesses. Absolutely nothing will harm you as you walk in this authority.

It's time to use your authority to cast the devil out of your home!

CHAPTER 2

GOD WARNS US

ABOUT CURSED OBJECTS

Whomen I was growing up, my parents warned me not to cross the street without looking both ways, not to take candy from strangers, not to forget to put on sunscreen before going to the beach—usually, they did that for us—and so on and so on and so on.

Our parents didn't warn us to keep us from getting to our friend's house faster, to deprive us of our favorite candy, or keep us from splashing in the water. No, they warned us because they knew if we crossed the street without looking both ways we could get run over by a car. They knew if we took candy from a stranger we could get kidnapped. And they knew going to the beach without sunscreen could leave us with painful burns.

In other words, love warns. Throughout the pages of the Bible, we see God warning us about danger. While there's no chapter and verse about the sunscreen or the candy, there are clear warnings of danger. God warned Noah of the coming flood that would destroy the earth (see Heb.

11:7). God sent angels to warn Lot and his family to get out of Sodom and Gomorrah before He rained fire and brimstone on the ancient cities (see Gen. 19).

Joseph, the earthly father of Jesus, was warned three times in three separate dreams not to go to certain places because doing so would but the baby Savior at risk. Jesus warned about false prophets, the leaven of religious Pharisees, greed, the devil, hypocrisy, pride, and the like.

Paul the apostle warned the believers in Galatia not to practice the works of the flesh or they would not inherit the Kingdom of God (see Gal. 5:19-21). In fact, Paul offered many warnings about the wages of sinful behavior, which is death (see Rom. 6:23).

A warning is an alert—it's the cry of wisdom to help you avert the danger of evil. A warning is strategic counsel to help you escape the wiles of the wicked. It's information that dispels ignorance. It's calling your attention to something that could harm you so that you can go a different direction.

THE DEVIL'S DARING SNARES

The devil uses snares to trap us—and many people are unknowingly trapped even now. The enemy works to trap us in sin through strategic temptations custom-made to leverage our weaknesses. Sometimes our weaknesses are home décor that carry demonic powers or music that seems harmless but subliminally renews our mind to evil.

The Bible has plenty to say about snares. A snare aims to entangle us. Put another way, a snare ties us up or puts us in bondage. Satan is sneaky with his snares. In spiritual warfare, you are not walking into a net that scoops you up and dangles you from a tree branch in a forest. No, in spiritual warfare the snares are invisible to the naked eye but clearly avoidable by the spiritually discerning.

God told the Israelites the gods of foreign nations would be snares to them (see Judg. 2:3). Translated into 21st-century language, that means demon powers set deceptively attractive traps to capture our souls. Psalm 106:36 plainly tells us idols are a snare to us. While an idol can be anything we place ahead of God—entertainment, money, people, etc.— in the days when Jehovah shared this revelation He was talking about statues people made by hand to worship. Demons are attracted to idols.

David said, "Those also who seek my life lay snares for me" (Ps. 38:12). David was dealing with flesh and blood enemies. We are dealing with demon powers. His enemies were talking in secret. David said, "They talk of laying snares secretly; they say, 'Who will see them?'" (Ps. 64:5). The enemy is counting on you not seeing his snares. After all, they don't always look like snares. You wouldn't knowingly bring a snare into your home.

Sometimes, snares come in the form of board games, graphic T-shirts, stuffed animals, and jewelry for which we pay good money or receive as gifts from friends and family. When someone suggests we should get rid of our snares, it offends our minds. After all, how could that cute little lizard do any harm? It just doesn't add up to many believers. That's because we have natural minds instead of spiritual minds. Or, put another way, our mind has not been renewed in that area because we haven't had any teaching on the topic. Paul told the believers in Corinth:

But people who aren't spiritual can't receive these truths from God's Spirit. It all sounds foolish to them and they can't understand it, for only those who are spiritual can understand what the Spirit means. Those who are spiritual can evaluate all things, but they themselves cannot be evaluated by others (1 Corinthians 2:14-15 NLT).

The enemy wants us to willingly walk into his snares and find ourselves trapped in his net by our own feet (see Job 18:8). And sometimes we do. Sometimes we willingly walk into a snare not out of ignorance but because we rejected the warning as foolishness. James 1:22-25 warns us:

But don't just listen to God's word. You must do what it says. Otherwise, you are only fooling yourselves. For if you listen to the word and don't obey, it is like glancing at your face in a mirror. You see yourself, walk away, and forget what you look like. But if you look carefully into the perfect law that sets you free, and if you do what it says and don't forget what you heard, then God will bless you for doing it (NLT).

GOD'S REPEATED WARNINGS ABOUT ACCURSED OBJECTS

In His great love He has for us, God always warns us of danger like any good father would. God warns us in His Word and He warns us by His Spirit when we are about to sin. This is called conviction. He warns us before we enter into bad relationships. He warns us not to go certain places and do certain things.

God also warns us about snares. God sees the enemy's snares before we see them, and even if we never see them. He tries to warn us. In fact, I know He tried to warn us before we brought accursed objects into our homes. He not only tried to warn us through the Word, which we'll look at in a moment, but He also tried to warn us through the promptings of the Holy Spirit. The problem is, sometimes we don't know the Word and sometimes we don't recognize the Holy Spirit's promptings.

God knows the enemy disguises himself and we can be deceived by the spirit of the world. Paul told us plainly that satan himself "masquerades as an angel of light" (2 Cor. 11:14 AMPC). *The Message* says satan is "dressing up as a beautiful angel of light." You've heard it said that the devil doesn't come knocking on your door dressed in a red suit with horns and a pitchfork. But we know he does crouch at our door with sin in his pocket waiting for you to invite him in. He comes in through the form of beautiful artwork, vases, statues, and other accursed objects.

God warns us over and over again in Scripture about the danger of accursed objects. If He had warned us just once, that would have been mercy. But He warns us over and over and over again. And He doesn't just warn us. He gives us horrifying illustrations of what happens to those who keep accursed objects in their possession. Consider these verses:

> *You shall burn the carved images of their gods with fire; you*
> *shall not covet the silver or gold that is on them, nor take it for*
> *yourselves, lest you be snared by it; for it is an abomination to*

the Lord your God. Nor shall you bring an abomination into your house, lest you be doomed to destruction like it. You shall utterly detest it and utterly abhor it, for it is an accursed thing (Deuteronomy 7:25-26).

And again:

So none of the accursed things shall remain in your hand, that the Lord may turn from the fierceness of His anger and show you mercy, have compassion on you and multiply you, just as He swore to your fathers, because you have listened to the voice of the Lord your God, to keep all His commandments which I command you today, to do what is right in the eyes of the Lord your God (Deuteronomy 13:17-18).

WHAT ACCURSED REALLY MEANS

What, exactly, is accursed? *Accursed* means being under or as if under a curse, according to *Merriam-Webster*'s dictionary. The Hebrew word for *accursed* in this verse is *charam*. It means "something devoted to destruction, banned, prohibited," according to *The KJV Old Testament Hebrew Lexicon*.

The Noah Webster 1828 Dictionary, which draws heavily from Scripture, defines *accursed* as "doomed to destruction or misery" and cites Joshua 7:17. He also defines it as "worthy of the curse, detestable, execrable" and cites Joshua 6:18. Finally, he defines it as wicked— malignant to the extreme.

I like the use of the word *malignant* there. When a doctor biopsies a growth on a patient's body, they are examining the cells to determine if they are benign or malignant. *Malignant* means something that produces death or deterioration; evil in nature, influence, or effect; injurious; and aggressively malicious, according to *Merriam-Webster's* dictionary. When the doctor says the growth is malignant, it's cancerous. Bringing accursed objects into your home is like smoking cigarettes—defiling your temple and inviting evil to wreak havoc on your life.

Accursed objects can come from accursed places. This is why I am careful not to bring back tokens from certain countries I visit. People have given me gifts that I have had to leave behind in hotel trash bins because, although they meant well and were trying to bless me, the gift basket had accursed objects. I could not take them into my home.

"We are in danger of having fellowship with the works of darkness if we take pleasure in fellowship with those who do such works," we find in *Matthew Henry's Concise Commentary*. "Whatever brings us into a snare, brings us under a curse. Let us be constant to our duty, and we cannot question the constancy of God's mercy."

No God-fearing Christian would knowingly bring accursed objects into their home. The devil is clever and crafty. He disguises evil in compelling packages. Designs on silverware, etchings in wood-carved art, and symbols on keychains are some of the ways we unknowingly bring accursed things in our homes. Ignorance is not bliss, but rather gives the devil rights to bring curses into your life.

ACHAN WAS WARNED

God spoke to Joshua and assured him of victory in the battles he faced. In Joshua 1:5-6, God assured him:

> *No man shall be able to stand before you all the days of your life; as I was with Moses, so I will be with you. I will not leave you nor forsake you. Be strong and of good courage, for to this people you shall divide as an inheritance the land which I swore to their fathers to give them.*

What a promise! I know God is with all of us. But if God was ever with anyone, He was with Moses. God spoke to Moses face to face! God showed Moses His glory. God worked miracles, signs, and wonders through the hands of Moses. What confidence must have sprung up in Joshua's heart when the Lord uttered those precious words to him.

Five chapters after he spoke those words, Jehovah gave Joshua a spiritual warfare strategy that included marching around the walled city of Jericho once a day for six days, then seven times on the seventh day. The strategy culminated with everyone shouting on the seventh day. You know the rest of the story. The walls came crashing down and Israel invaded the city. The Lord told Joshua the city was doomed for destruction. This was a brilliant victory, which sure gave Joshua even more confidence in the Lord's leadership.

Immediately after offering the breakthrough spiritual warfare strategy, God told Joshua:

And you, by all means abstain from the accursed things, lest you become accursed when you take of the accursed things, and make the camp of Israel a curse, and trouble it. But all the silver and gold, and vessels of bronze and iron, are consecrated to the Lord; they shall come into the treasury of the Lord (Joshua 6:18-19).

The Message puts it this way,

As for you, watch yourselves in the city under holy curse. Be careful that you don't covet anything in it and take something that's cursed, endangering the camp of Israel with the curse and making trouble for everyone. All silver and gold, all vessels of bronze and iron are holy to God. Put them in God's treasury.

WHEN YOUR WHOLE HOUSE SUFFERS

Joshua heard the warning loud and clear, as did the other Israelites. Apparently, that serious warning went in one of Achan's ears and out the other. Despite the sober warning and the miraculous victory at Jericho, Achan could not resist the temptation to take some of the accursed things for himself.

But the children of Israel committed a trespass regarding the accursed things, for Achan the son of Carmi, the son of Zabdi, the son of Zerah, of the tribe of Judah, took of the accursed things; so the anger of the Lord burned against the children of Israel (Joshua 7:1).

We don't like to think of God as angry, but He was. The New Living Translation says "the Lord was very angry with the Israelites."

Catch that. Only Achan sinned. He was the only one who disobeyed the Lord's command. The only one. Achan's sin brought negative consequences for the entire nation of Israel. That doesn't seem fair to the natural mind. But God saw the nation of Israel as one unit. You may not have brought any accursed things into your home, but if someone else who lives with you has brought in cursed objects, you will feel the sting. God sees your household, in this respect, as the family unit.

Unfortunately, Joshua had no idea Achan brought evil spirits back into the camp. (Idols are representative of demons and carry evil spirits.) He had a mighty victory against Jericho and was ready to drive out more of God's enemies from the Promised Land according to the Joshua 1:5-6 promise God gave him. What happens next is absolutely tragic.

When it was time to advance again, Joshua did not hesitate. He sent up a small crew, about three thousand men, to go up against Ai. But Ai's army struck down a good number of Israelites, seemingly defying the promise Jehovah made to the young warrior. Joshua didn't understand it. He couldn't figure it out. God had told him He would be with him wherever he went, just like He was with Moses. So where was God in this battle? Why didn't God tell Joshua not to go up? The disobedience of one man grieved the Holy Spirit. Joshua began to mourn. What happens in Joshua 7:10-13 is a lesson for us all.

So the Lord said to Joshua: "Get up! Why do you lie thus on your face? Israel has sinned, and they have also transgressed My covenant which I commanded them. For they have even taken some of the accursed things, and have both stolen and deceived; and they have also put it among their own stuff. Therefore the children of Israel could not stand before their enemies, but turned their backs before their enemies, because they have become doomed to destruction. Neither will I be with you anymore, unless you destroy the accursed from among you. Get up, sanctify the people, and say, 'Sanctify yourselves for tomorrow, because thus says the Lord God of Israel: "There is an accursed thing in your midst, O Israel; you cannot stand before your enemies until you take away the accursed thing from among you."'"

GOD MAKES AN EXAMPLE OF ACHAN

This was news to Joshua. It must have been a shocker. I can almost see his jaw dropping in disbelief. Achan disobeyed God, but Joshua didn't know it. Again, people who live in your house may be opening your home up to demonization with the objects they bring in or the media they consume within your walls. Sometimes, this is totally innocent. Other times, roommates, spouses, and children are reading books, wearing clothing, or otherwise engaging in rebellion that invites demons into your home.

You have to get to the root of the issue, like God helped Joshua do. God told him:

> *In the morning therefore you shall be brought according to your tribes. And it shall be that the tribe which the Lord takes shall come according to families; and the family which the Lord takes shall come by households; and the household which the Lord takes shall come man by man. Then it shall be that he who is taken with the accursed thing shall be burned with fire, he and all that he has, because he has transgressed the covenant of the Lord, and because he has done a disgraceful thing in Israel* (Joshua 7:14-15).

Joshua followed God's instructions step by step. The next morning he brought Israel out tribe by tribe. I can feel the suspense in the air and even the fear of the Lord as the tribes were winnowed. First, Judah was singled out. Next, the clans within the tribe of Judah came forward, and the clan called Zerah was singled out. Next, the families of Zerah came forward, and the family of Zimri was singled out. Finally, Zimri's entire family was brought forth one by one. And there was Achan, exposed. What happens next is startling.

> *Now Joshua said to Achan, "My son, I beg you, give glory to the Lord God of Israel, and make confession to Him, and tell me now what you have done; do not hide it from me." And Achan answered Joshua and said, "Indeed I have sinned against the Lord God of Israel, and this is what I have done: When I saw among the spoils a beautiful Babylonian garment, two hundred shekels of silver, and a wedge of gold weighing fifty shekels, I*

coveted them and took them. And there they are, hidden in the earth in the midst of my tent, with the silver under it" (Joshua 7:19-21).

Joshua sent messengers, who indeed found a Babylonian garment, two hundred shekels of silver, and fifty shekels of gold hidden in the ground under his tent. Notice two things here. First, Achan knew what he did was wrong, but he did it anyway and caused the loss of life among the Israelite soldiers. Second, he hid the accursed objects. We may not hide the accursed objects in our homes—they may be on open display on our bookshelves as knickknacks. But know this: demons are hiding on accursed objects.

Then Joshua, and all Israel with him, took Achan the son of Zerah, the silver, the garment, the wedge of gold, his sons, his daughters, his oxen, his donkeys, his sheep, his tent, and all that he had, and they brought them to the Valley of Achor. And Joshua said, "Why have you troubled us? The Lord will trouble you this day." So all Israel stoned him with stones; and they burned them with fire after they had stoned them with stones (Joshua 7:24-25).

Noteworthy is the fact that *Jones' Dictionary of Old Testament Proper Names* gives a sinister meaning for *Achan*—"serpent." Other scholars argue it means "troublemaker," but Achan comes from a Hebrew word that means "serpent." And there's only one Achan in the Bible like there's only one satan in the Bible. The spirit of Achan tempts us to bring accursed objects into our home, sometimes by the beauty of the object or its desirability in some other form.

Achan was not punished alone for the accursed objects. His whole family paid the price. Of course, God is not going to kill you if you have cursed objects in your home. But I can't stress this enough. The enemy works through accursed objects to kill destinies, destroy health, and steal what belongs to you through the curse it carries. When someone brings a cursed object into your home, it affects not just the one who brought it in but everyone in the home—even if you don't know it's there. I'll say it again, ignorance is not bliss.

MICAH'S STOLEN IDOLS

The story of Achan is sad, but there's an equally sad—and telling—story tucked away in the Old Testament. In the pages of the Book of Judges, which most often speaks of the exploits of the judges God used to free Israel from enemy bondage after a period of judgment, we find the unusual story of Micah. He was a man from the mountains of Ephraim who apparently didn't learn from the sin of Achan, which doubtless was notorious in Israel's history.

> He said to his mother, "The eleven hundred shekels of silver that were taken from you, and on which you put a curse, even saying it in my ears—here is the silver with me; I took it." And his mother said, "May you be blessed by the Lord, my son!" (Judges 17:2)

Like Achan, Micah confessed his sin but that didn't do away with the curse, which quite literally was on the person who took the coins as well as on the coins themselves.

Put another way, Micah's mother probably got angry when the coins—a considerable sum—were found missing and cursed the one who took them. Micah overheard his mother releasing this curse and perhaps finally remembered Achan's sin. Even as a few of the coins rattled around in his pocket, he got nervous and decided to fess up to mama, falling on her mercy.

The New King James Version says she blessed her son, but in reality the New Living Translation is a little more telling: "The Lord bless you for admitting it." His mother did not absolve his guilt. She didn't utter words of forgiveness. She was just glad to get the coins back, but she didn't ask the Lord to remove the curse either. So now she had a cursed son and cursed coins. Together, they decided to make them into an idol. Read the account.

> So when he had returned the eleven hundred shekels of silver to his mother, his mother said, "I had wholly dedicated the silver from my hand to the Lord for my son, to make a carved image and a molded image; now therefore, I will return it to you." Thus he returned the silver to his mother. Then his mother took two hundred shekels of silver and gave them to the silversmith, and he made it into a carved image and a molded image; and they were in the house of Micah.
>
> The man Micah had a shrine, and made an ephod and household idols; and he consecrated one of his sons, who became

his priest. In those days there was no king in Israel; everyone did what was right in his own eyes (Judges 17:3-6).

THE CURSE CAUSELESS?

You've heard it said a curse causeless shall not land. That comes from Proverbs 26:2. The New Living Translation says, "An undeserved curse will not land on its intended victim." *The Passion Translation* says, "An undeserved curse will be powerless to harm you." But bringing accursed objects into our homes willingly—even if unknowingly—is cause enough to snare you. There was a cause for the curse Micah would soon realize was on his life.

Indeed, what happens next is amazing. A Levite comes to Micah's house and the coin-stealing idol worshiper asks him to be a father and a priest to him in exchange for ten pieces of silver every year, a suit of clothes, and any other living expenses. The Levite gladly takes him up on the offer.

After some time, five members of Israel's tribe of Dan come along and ask Micah's priest for warfare advice. Micah's priest essentially prophesied a good word to them: "Go in peace. The presence of the Lord be with you on your way." The Danites succeeded in battle and must have given some of the credit to the Levite because they decided he should be a permanent fixture in their tribe. They decided to take the priest from Micah. They went to the priest's house with six hundred warriors.

The Danites took the carved image, the ephod, the household idols, and the molded image. The priest objected, but the Danites told him to be quiet and go with them:

> *"Is it better for you to be a priest to the household of one man, or that you be a priest to a tribe and a family in Israel?" So the priest's heart was glad; and he took the ephod, the household idols, and the carved image, and took his place among the people* (Judges 18:19-20).

Suddenly, the priest whom Micah thought was a blessing turned into a curse. The curse was latent for some period of time, but not impotent. The curse would manifest at an opportune time. The opportune time had arrived. Micah didn't take the news lying down. He went after his priest. He protested:

> *"You have taken away my gods which I made, and the priest, and you have gone away. Now what more do I have? How can you say to me, 'What ails you?'"*
>
> *And the children of Dan said to him, "Do not let your voice be heard among us, lest angry men fall upon you, and you lose your life, with the lives of your household!" Then the children of Dan went their way. And when Micah saw that they were too strong for him, he turned and went back to his house* (Judges 18:24-26).

At first, the Danites were successful in their conquests with the priest and Micah's idols. But the curse would manifest in the Danite camp at an opportune time in the future. Micah didn't know it at the time, but the Danites did him a favor by taking the cursed objects from his home. Micah was now curse-free. Eventually, the land the Danites occupied went into captivity. This is why, as we'll explain later, when you cleanse your home from evil, you do not want to give the objects away or donate them to any organization. You could pass the curse on to an unsuspecting individual.

NO BLOOD ON MY HANDS

I write this book as a watchman. (You can also read my book *The Making of a Watchman*.) The Lord compelled me to give you warning from Him. It's never comfortable to do so. I am not your judge. I'm just the messenger. Indeed, God wants to use me as a deliverer in your home if you'll let me. See, God called me as a watchman many years ago and I take it seriously. He called me from Ezekiel 3. I was in Nicaragua at the time when the Lord told me to open these chapters. Ezekiel 3:17-21 reads:

> *Son of man, I have made you a watchman for the house of Israel; therefore hear a word from My mouth, and give them warning from Me: When I say to the wicked, "You shall surely die," and you give him no warning, nor speak to warn the wicked from his wicked way, to save his life, that same wicked man shall die in his iniquity; but his blood I will require at your hand. Yet, if you warn the wicked, and he does not turn from his wickedness, nor from his wicked way, he shall die in his iniquity; but you have delivered your soul.*

Again, when a righteous man turns from his righteousness and commits iniquity, and I lay a stumbling block before him, he shall die; because you did not give him warning, he shall die in his sin, and his righteousness which he has done shall not be remembered; but his blood I will require at your hand. Nevertheless if you warn the righteous man that the righteous should not sin, and he does not sin, he shall surely live because he took warning; also you will have delivered your soul.

Perhaps because I wasn't getting it, God sent me thirty chapters down the line to Ezekiel 33. I started reading in verse one and the storyline got more intense. Ezekiel 33:1-9 shook me:

Again the word of the Lord came to me, saying, "Son of man, speak to the children of your people, and say to them: 'When I bring the sword upon a land, and the people of the land take a man from their territory and make him their watchman, when he sees the sword coming upon the land, if he blows the trumpet and warns the people, then whoever hears the sound of the trumpet and does not take warning, if the sword comes and takes him away, his blood shall be on his own head. He heard the sound of the trumpet, but did not take warning; his blood shall be upon himself. But he who takes warning will save his life. But if the watchman sees the sword coming and does not blow the trumpet, and the people are not warned, and the sword comes and takes any person from among them, he is taken away in his iniquity; but his blood I will require at the watchman's hand.'

"So you, son of man: I have made you a watchman for the house of Israel; therefore you shall hear a word from My mouth and warn them for Me. When I say to the wicked, 'O wicked man, you shall surely die!' and you do not speak to warn the wicked from his way, that wicked man shall die in his iniquity; but his blood I will require at your hand. Nevertheless if you warn the wicked to turn from his way, and he does not turn from his way, he shall die in his iniquity; but you have delivered your soul."

THIS IS YOUR WARNING

I realize you won't like some of what is written on these pages. Remember, there is no condemnation in Christ. I am not suggesting you do something I haven't done myself more than once. Please, consider this your love warning. I don't want blood on my hands and you don't want a curse on your household. We both win.

God is warning you through the pages of this book to go through your home and find the accursed objects. Proverbs 29:6 warns, "By transgression an evil man is snared, but the righteous sings and rejoices." While all sin is a snare, bringing idols into your home is akin to inviting demons into your home.

While you can easily repent of gossiping or slander and be washed white as snow, the idols—or accursed objects—you bring into your home have to be cast out. In other words, you can't just repent for bringing an accursed object in your home. You have to cleanse your home from evil.

Peter warned the devil is roaming about like a roaring lion seeking someone to devour—and sometimes he's doing it from within your house through cursed objects and sinful habits that open the door wide for the enemy to squat in your house. The good news is, even if you have fallen into a snare, He can and will deliver you (see Ps. 91:3).

I am not trying to convince you to throw away things you or your children love or have fun with to make you miserable. I am trying to reveal to you how some things in your home may be making you miserable. As you read the pages of this book, you will see things in a new way and it will lead you into a righteous indignation that will cause you to rise up and cleanse your home of evil. In Paul's letter to the believers at Corinth, he shared some hard truths, but it was for the deliverance of the church:

> *For even if I made you sorry with my letter, I do not regret it; though I did regret it. For I perceive that the same epistle made you sorry, though only for a while. Now I rejoice, not that you were made sorry, but that your sorrow led to repentance. For you were made sorry in a godly manner, that you might suffer loss from us in nothing.*
>
> *For godly sorrow produces repentance leading to salvation, not to be regretted; but the sorrow of the world produces death. For observe this very thing, that you sorrowed in a godly manner: What diligence it produced in you, what clearing of yourselves, what indignation, what fear, what vehement desire, what zeal, what vindication! In all things you proved yourselves to be clear in this matter.*

Therefore, although I wrote to you, I did not do it for the sake of him who had done the wrong, nor for the sake of him who suffered wrong, but that our care for you in the sight of God might appear to you (2 Corinthians 7:8-12).

That's my angle with this book. To help you see the enemy's plan, disavow it, repent to God for participating in it, and show you how to reverse the curses, in Jesus' name!

CHAPTER 3

13 SIGNS YOU

HAVE CURSED OBJECTS IN YOUR HOME

L*et's Make a Deal* was a wildly popular American television game show in the 1960s. Monty Hall served as its host for a whopping thirty years. Maybe you've seen it. In case you haven't, here's how it worked: Monty walked into the studio audience with his thin microphone and asked someone to stand up and give their name and where they are from. Dubbed "traders," the people Monty picked would negotiate with the host.

Many times, Monty started out by asking the trader to produce something they were carrying with them, say, with their name on it, in exchange for a small prize of a few dollars. That was usually an easy deal to make. When the trader cooperated, he offered another challenge, such as, "Tell me how many letters are in your name in ten seconds" in exchange for an even greater monetary prize. The trader wins the prize and is on a roll.

Then the temptations start. Monty might bring out a big box, wrapped neatly with a colorful ribbon, and present it to that trader. Monty lets the trader choose to keep their current loot or trade it in for what's in the box—sight unseen. At least some of the time, the trader decides to gamble what is in their hand that they can see for what's in the box that they can't see. In one episode, a lady traded the $30 for the fur coat. What a blessing! The studio audience goes wild.

Now that the audience sees success from the first trader, Monty ups the stakes. He finds a new trader, who watches as a curtain pulls back to reveal a brand-new car and gives her the keys. She's overwhelmed with excitement. Monty asks the trader, for example, what is the name for the mileage indicator as written in the car's manual. She has ten seconds to answer. She thinks and thinks—and thinks. The woman gets the answer wrong and has to give back the keys.

Monty gives her another chance. He names a subject and she gets to ask him any question on the subject. If he can't answer, she gets what's in the bright red box. She asks and he can't answer. She wins, and he puts a twist on the contest. He tells her she can take what's in his top coat pocket or what's in the box. She chooses the box. Inside the box is a child's play toy. Inside his pocket was $50, the better choice.

As the show goes on, the stakes get higher. People have made some serious errors in choosing on the show. There were blessings in abundance in their hand, but they traded it because they were tempted. Some people lost cars to receive a disappointing deal, such as live sheep, fur covered garbage cans, play money, and junky old furniture. They knew they were taking a risk. But they decided to trade the blessing for a booby prize.

WHAT ARE YOU CHOOSING?

Like Monty gives the traders a choice, God gave the Israelites a choice—and He gives us a choice. If you had a choice, you would choose blessings over curses—life over death. Who wouldn't, right? Every day, we have to make decisions on how we think, how we behave—and what we choose to bring in our homes. What looks like a blessing can be a curse. In Deuteronomy 30:15-19, God gives the Israelites a warning we would do well to heed:

> *See, I have set before you today life and good, death and evil, in that I command you today to love the Lord your God, to walk in His ways, and to keep His commandments, His statutes, and His judgments, that you may live and multiply; and the Lord your God will bless you in the land which you go to possess.*

> *But if your heart turns away so that you do not hear, and are drawn away, and worship other gods and serve them, I announce to you today that you shall surely perish; you shall not prolong your days in the land which you cross over the Jordan to go in and possess. I call heaven and earth as witnesses today against you, that I have set before you life and death, blessing and cursing; therefore choose life, that both you and your descendants may live.*

So I ask you again, what are you choosing? Blessings or curses? You could be the model Christian, doing your daily devotions, praying, serving in your church, paying your tithes, and the like. But if you are choosing to bring accursed objects into your home, you will eventually pay a price you don't want to pay. Bringing accursed objects into your home brings the curses of disobedience into our lives.

Deuteronomy 28 offers a lengthy list of the blessings of obedience and the curses associated with disobedience. In your disobedience to the Lord, the enemy will try to bring these curses upon your life. I believe the grace of God is wider than we think. We don't have a license to sin, but God is not going to allow the enemy to bring permanent curses in our lives over one mistake. This is why we need to be quick to repent and cleanse our home from evil.

So what are the signs of the curse working over your life? Pulling from Deuteronomy 28, we can see biblical signs of curses. Mind you, it's not necessary for you to experience all of the below as evidence of a curse. Any one of these issues may be the manifestation of a curse. If you see any of these things operating in your life, what harm would it do to go through your home to see if there is an accursed object? A small time investment could break the curse and restore God's highest blessings on your life.

1. You are not prosperous.

God's will is for you to prosper and be in health, even as your soul prospers (see 3 John 1:2). He gives us the power to create wealth to establish His covenant in the earth (see Deut. 8:18). He promises to supply all of our needs according to His riches in glory in Christ Jesus (see Phil. 4:19).

God tells us when we sow our tithes and offerings He will rebuke the devourer and open the windows of heaven to pour out a blessing we can't contain (see Mal. 3:10). We know the blessing of the Lord makes us rich and He adds no sorry to it (see Prov. 10:22). God's will is for us to prosper in everything we put our hand to.

So if you are not prosperous, there's a problem somewhere. It could be that you are a poor steward of what He has put in your hand. It could be that you are under spiritual attack and need to learn how to fight back. It could be that you have a poverty mentality and lack in your mouth. But it could also be the sign of a curse.

Deuteronomy 28:16-19 ties disobedience to your fields, your fruit baskets and breadboards, and crops will be cursed. It also points to poverty among your children, the offspring of your herds and flocks. Deuteronomy 28:38-39,42 continues:

> *You will plant much but harvest little, for locusts will eat your crops. You will plant vineyards and care for them, but you will not drink the wine or eat the grapes, for worms will destroy the vines. ...Swarms of insects will destroy your trees and crops* (NLT).

All of this is connected to your prosperity. When you change jobs hoping for a better lot, you fail. Instead of the Midas touch, everything you touch seems to fall apart. No matter what you try, it doesn't succeed. Again, the Bible says everything you put your hand to shall prosper, but when nothing is prospering there could be a hidden curse on your life.

2. Confusion and frustration.

God is not the author of confusion but of peace (see 1 Cor. 14:33). Likewise, God is not the author of frustration but of grace. Grace is a gift that empowers us to do what God has called us to do. Grace is also the unmerited favor of God. We know God resists the proud, for example, and gives grace to the humble (see James 4:6). Grace is a blessing. We can't earn it, but God can withhold it.

Continual confusion and persistent frustration in your life are signs that curses may be present. If you can't seem to get clarity on God's will, feel you are wandering around in the wilderness, or hit continual obstacles without seeing breakthrough, there could be a curse in place. Deuteronomy 28:20 says, "The Lord himself will send on you curses, confusion, and frustration in everything you do, until at last you are completely destroyed for doing evil and abandoning me" (NLT). That's a heavy word!

3. Sickness and disease.

God wants you to walk in divine health. Echoing Isaiah's prophecy, First Peter 2:24 tells us Jesus "bore our sins in His own body on the tree, that we, having died to sins, might live for righteousness—by whose stripes you were healed." When Jesus walked the earth, He healed every disease and every affliction among the people (see Matt. 4:23).

God's will has always been to heal. The psalmist said, "Bless the Lord, O my soul, and forget not all His benefits: who forgives all your iniquities, who heals all your diseases" (Ps. 103:2-3). Even before the list of blessings and curses in Deuteronomy 28, God told the Israelites in Exodus 15:26, "If you diligently heed the voice of the Lord your God and do what is right in His sight, give ear to His commandments and keep all His statutes, I will put none of the diseases on you which I have brought on the Egyptians. For I am the Lord who heals you."

We open the door to the enemy—and give him a right to bring sickness and disease in our lives—through disobedience. When you have accursed objects in your home, you have given the enemy what I call proximity. The enemy is close and the disobedience is ongoing. As long as you keep the accursed object in your house, you have an open door. Deuteronomy 28:21-22 says:

> *The Lord will afflict you with diseases until none of you are left in the land you are about to enter and occupy. The Lord will strike you with wasting diseases, fever, and inflammation, with scorching heat and drought, and with blight and mildew. These disasters will pursue you until you die* (NLT).

And Deuteronomy 28:27 adds, "The Lord will afflict you with the boils of Egypt and with tumors, scurvy, and the itch, from which you cannot be cured" (NLT). And again, Deuteronomy 28:35, "The Lord will cover your knees and legs with incurable boils. In fact, you will be covered from head to foot" (NLT). If you are plagued with sickness and disease, work to cleanse your home from any evil.

4. You are in famine.

Jesus gave us an eternal truth in John 10:10, "The thief comes only in order to steal and kill and destroy. I came that they may have and enjoy life, and have it in abundance (to the full, till it overflows)" (AMPC). God wants you to live a life of abundance. He wants you to enjoy your life and live in the overflow. David said his cup was overflowing (see Ps. 23:5). Yours should be too.

Our heavenly Father is a God of abundance. We know that He is able to do far more abundantly than anything we ask or think. Inspired by the Holy Spirit, David told us, "The Lord knows the days of the upright, and their inheritance shall be forever. They shall not be ashamed in the evil time, and in the days of famine they shall be satisfied" (Ps. 37:18-19).

Lacking prosperity is one thing; famine is another. Some curses take you into famine, which is extreme scarcity. Deuteronomy 28:24 reads, "The Lord will change the rain that falls on your land into powder, and dust will pour down from the sky until you are destroyed" (NLT). Throughout Scripture we see famines, which are signs of a curse. Even in a natural famine, it's possible for the obedient to prosper. Remember, Jacob sowed in the land of famine and received a hundredfold return that same year.

If you are in famine—whether a financial famine, a famine of joy, a famine of peace, a famine of friends or any other type of famine—consider the root. Could there be an accursed object in your home? Take the time to find out.

5. You are under constant attack.

Everyone has seasons of warfare—even extreme warfare. But even David, the mighty warrior, had seasons of rest from war. When the warfare won't cease, there could be a curse in place.

> *The Lord will cause you to be defeated by your enemies. You will attack your enemies from one direction, but you will scatter from them in seven! You will be an object of horror to all the kingdoms of the earth. Your corpses will be food*

for all the scavenging birds and wild animals, and no one will be there to chase them away (Deuteronomy 28:25-26 NLT).

We see this playing out over and over again in Judges. Judges 2:14 recalls, "And the anger of the Lord was hot against Israel. So He delivered them into the hands of plunderers who despoiled them; and He sold them into the hands of their enemies all around, so that they could no longer stand before their enemies."

James, the apostle of practical faith, told us to submit to God, resist the devil, and he will flee (see James 4:7). When you have an accursed object in your house, the devil has a legal right. You are not submitted to God in this area and the devil doesn't have to flee because you invited him in.

6. Mental health issues and oppression will arise.

God has promised to keep us in perfect peace if we keep our eyes on Him (see Isa. 26:3). Jesus left us His very own peace, and the Spirit of Peace—the Holy Spirit—dwells on the inside of us.

When we are struggling in our minds, something is wrong; we have either looked away from the Lord or we haven't cast our cares on Him, or we're not thinking the right thoughts, or we haven't cast down imaginations—or there is a curse somewhere.

Mental health issues might not be a chemical imbalance. Oppression can stem from curses. Deuteronomy 28:28 reads, "The Lord will strike you with madness, blindness, and panic" (NLT). And Deuteronomy 28:33-34 adds, "You will suffer under constant oppression and harsh treatment. You will go mad because of all the tragedy you see around you" (NLT). The New King James Version says, "So you shall be driven mad because of the sight which your eyes see."

Remember Nebuchadnezzar? The king of Babylon was not in covenant with the Lord, but his insistence on worshiping idols—even worshiping himself—drove him crazy. Nebuchadnezzar lost his mind: "He was driven from men and ate grass like oxen; his body was wet with the dew of heaven till his hair had grown like eagles' feathers and his nails like birds' claws" (Dan. 4:33).

The good news is Nebuchadnezzar was restored, and so was his kingdom, when he repented. If your emotional issues stem from a curse over your life, you can cast the devil out of your house and get your mind back.

7. People will take what is yours.

Jesus told us the thief comes to steal, kill, and destroy (see John 10:10). Sometimes he uses people to do it. The enemy has a right when you give him one. One sign of being under a curse is people stealing, killing, or destroying what belongs to you or what you love.

Where a curse is present, you may find people will meddle with your money, your property, your friends, your spouse, and more. Specifically, Deuteronomy 28:30-33 reads:

You will be engaged to a woman, but another man will sleep with her. You will build a house, but someone else will live in it. You will plant a vineyard, but you will never enjoy its fruit.

Your ox will be butchered before your eyes, but you will not eat a single bite of the meat.

Your donkey will be taken from you, never to be returned. Your sheep and goats will be given to your enemies, and no one will be there to help you. You will watch as your sons and daughters are taken away as slaves. Your heart will break for them, but you won't be able to help them. A foreign nation you have never heard about will eat the crops you worked so hard to grow (NLT).

Deuteronomy 28:41 adds, "You will have sons and daughters, but you will lose them, for they will be led away into captivity" (NLT).

What does this mean? Your marriage may come under severe attack and may be destroyed. Your home may come under fire. Your kids may fall into temptations that harm their soul, such as addictions, depression, or even turning away from the Lord completely. If you are noticing the enemy is pillaging what's personal to you, it's time to examine the root cause, which may be in your house.

8. You will be rejected.

Ephesians 1:6 tells us we are accepted in Christ. This is a promise and no curse can change that. But where a curse is present, the spirit of rejection may begin attacking your life on all fronts. People will imagine the worst about you because the enemy gives them evil thoughts about your motives. People will see you as less than—the tail and not the head.

The impacts of rejection can ripple through your life in perhaps unexpected ways. Science proves rejection can change your hormones, cause your physical body to ache—it can even impact your digestion. Researchers say rejection can literally make your heart hurt and your mind can go into withdrawal. Rejection can cause anxiety, depression, and brain fog.

Although there is a spirit of rejection that can be cast out, there is also a curse of rejection that has to be broken. Deuteronomy 28:37, "You will become an object of horror, ridicule, and mockery among all the nations to which the Lord sends you" (NLT).

If you are dealing with cycles of rejection and its ripples, it's worth exploring if the curse of rejection is on your life. Could it be possible you've brought something—or allowed something—into your home that is causing this cycle?

9. You live in fear.

The Word of God tells us over and over again not to fear. In fact, Paul told his spiritual son Timothy, "God has not given us a spirit of fear, but of power and of love and of a sound mind" (2 Tim. 1:7). John, the one who described himself as "the disciple Jesus loved" emphasized this truth: "There is no fear in love; but perfect love casts out fear, because fear involves torment. But he who fears has not been made perfect in love" (1 John 4:18).

All curses bring some measure of torment, but fear is one of the most insidious spirits roaming about. Torment is a hellish experience, and indeed those who land in hell will face torment (see Rev. 20:10). God has not called us to torment, but a curse—especially the curse of fear—can be tormenting. All of us feel fear from time to time, but when you are under a curse you may find yourself living in fear and unable to resist it.

And the Lord will cause your heart to tremble, your eyesight to fail, and your soul to despair. Your life will constantly hang in the balance. You will live night and day in fear, unsure if you will survive. In the morning you will say, "If only it were night!" And in the evening you will say, "If only it were morning!" For you will be terrified by the awful horrors you see around you (Deuteronomy 28:65-67 NLT).

When a curse lands on you, you may begin to operate in dread. A cousin of fear, dread makes you uneasy about facing day-to-day life. You don't expect good things anymore because so many bad things are happening to you. You become negative and pessimistic and speak words of death that further create problems in your life.

The Lord wants to deliver you from your fears, according to Psalm 34:4, but sometimes you have to break a curse to see that deliverance. Could the media, clothing, or other items that have found a comfortable place on your bookshelves be making room for the torment of fear? Investigate with the Holy Spirit and get ready for a newfound freedom.

10. Curses seem to chase you down.

When there are accursed objects in your home, you may begin to feel as if you are magnetized to attract curses. It seems you can't catch a break no matter how hard you try. You grow hopeless because hope deferred makes the heart sick (see Prov. 13:12). You stand on the brink of breakthrough only to find backlash before you bring yourself to the finish line.

Deuteronomy 28:19 says, "Wherever you go and whatever you do, you will be cursed" (NLT). Instead of blessings chasing you down and overtaking you, it seems bad things find you at every turn. The Contemporary English Version puts it this way, "The Lord will make you fail in everything you do."

Be sure the Lord is not cursing you, but it can feel that way. When we have accursed objects in our homes, we are essentially inviting the devil to squat on our premises. You can't serve him eviction papers until you discern where he's hiding. But once you find the accursed object, you can kick the devil out of your house.

11. You have no vision for your life.

Solomon put it plainly, "Where there is no vision, the people perish" (Prov. 29:18 KJV). The Amplified Bible, Classic Edition really makes this plain: "Where there is no vision [no redemptive revelation of God], the people perish." Even *The Passion Translation* can't put a positive spin on this one, reading: "When there is no clear prophetic vision, people quickly wander astray."

We need to see what the Father is doing in our lives so we can agree with it. We need to know where the Holy Spirit is going so we can follow His lead. But where a curse is present, we often find ourselves unable to see or hear like the idols we've brought into our home.

Deuteronomy 28:29 reads, "You will grope around in broad daylight like a blind person groping in the darkness, but you will not find your way" (NLT). So when curses are present, you may not be able to see where you are going. You are too overwhelmed to even think about purpose and destiny.

If you find yourself in this condition, don't stop seeking the Lord. He wants to help you. He wants to show you what the problem is. Be open to the idea that the problem could be something you brought into your home that is clouding your spiritual senses—and then go on a mission to get it out!

12. You lose your anointing.

You won't lose your salvation because you bring an accursed object into your house, but it can feel as if you've lost your anointing. Where you operated in a healing or prophetic ministry, it can seem like the rivers are not flowing anymore. I'm not talking about a dry season. I'm talking about enemy interference to your release.

Consider Deuteronomy 28:40, which reads, "You will grow olive trees throughout your land, but you will never use the olive oil, for the fruit will drop before it ripens" (NLT). The oil represents your anointing. When certain curses are present, you will find you are not walking in the power of the Holy Spirit. Be assured, the Holy Spirit has not left you. He wants to help you root out the antichrist spirits in your home through the items that may have found their way in—sometimes through no fault of your own.

13. Your prayers are not answered.

Where a curse is present, it can seem like your prayer life is dried up. You pray and pray and pray until there's nothing left to say but answers elude you. You know you are praying God's will and you know He hears you—at least in theory—but you start to doubt because you see little to no fruit of your prayer life.

Deuteronomy 28:23 says, "The skies above will be as unyielding as bronze, and the earth beneath will be as hard as iron" (NLT). This is a hard heaven, where your prayers hit a ceiling and fall to the ground. The principalities are blocking your prayers, but the angel armies are not coming to your aid like they did for Daniel because you have agreed with the dark forces of the second heaven.

I can assure you, though, God does hear your prayers and if you cry out for deliverance from evil—if you ask Him to help you cleanse your home from evil—He will. God is a very present help in time of trouble (see Ps. 46:1). God is not mad at you. He wants to help you kick the devil out of your house and walk in His highest blessing on your life.

UNLOCKING THE BLESSINGS OF GOD

I hope to further incentivize you to go on this journey with me not by focusing on the curse but by keeping your eyes on the prize—the blessings of God. The blessings of God are part of your inheritance in Christ. Legally, God has blessed you with every spiritual blessing (see Eph. 1:3). You may have to fight to see it manifest, but you are well able to cleanse your home from evil. Psalm 119:2 assures us we're blessed when we follow His ways and seek Him with our whole heart.

Here's what you can expect when you kick the devil out of your house. Read this over and again and let these verses inspire your heart to go on an expedition with the Holy Spirit and root out every accursed object. Deuteronomy 28:1-14 reads:

Now it shall come to pass, if you diligently obey the voice of the Lord your God, to observe carefully all His commandments which I command you today, that the Lord your God will set you high above all nations of the earth. And all these blessings shall come upon you and overtake you, because you obey the voice of the Lord your God:

Blessed shall you be in the city, and blessed shall you be in the country. Blessed shall be the fruit of your body, the produce of your ground and the increase of your herds, the increase of your cattle and the offspring of your flocks. Blessed shall be your basket and your kneading bowl. Blessed shall you be when you come in, and blessed shall you be when you go out. The Lord will cause your enemies who rise against you to be defeated before your face; they shall come out against you one way and flee before you seven ways. The Lord will command the blessing on you in your storehouses and in all to which you set your hand, and He will bless you in the land which the Lord your God is giving you.

The Lord will establish you as a holy people to Himself, just as He has sworn to you, if you keep the commandments of the Lord your God and walk in His ways. Then all peoples of the earth shall see that you are called by the name of the Lord, and they shall be afraid of you. And the Lord will grant you plenty of goods, in the fruit of your body, in the increase of your livestock, and in the produce of your ground, in the land of which the Lord swore to your fathers to give you.

The Lord will open to you His good treasure, the heavens, to give the rain to your land in its season, and to bless all the work of your hand. You shall lend to many nations, but you shall not borrow. And the Lord will make you the head and not the tail; you shall be above only, and not be beneath, if you heed the commandments of the Lord your God, which I command you today, and are careful to observe them. So you shall not turn aside from any of the words which I command you this day, to the right or the left, to go after other gods to serve them.

Are you ready to go on this journey with the Holy Spirit? Don't leave any stone unturned. Choose to be open-minded so the Holy Spirit can speak to your heart about what's hidden in darkness. As I always say, a devil exposed is a devil defeated. The rest of this book will help you expose the curse-makers so you can rise up and be a curse-breaker.

CHAPTER 4

NATIVE AMERICAN

SYMBOLOGY CAN ATTRACT EVIL

Florida, like some other states, is home to what are called Indian mounds—about 45 of them on record but there may be many more yet to be uncovered and some may have been built over. Indian mounds are burial sites for Native Americans. Natives architected Indian mounds with shell, soil, rock, and other materials hundreds of years ago. These mounds are home to *chindi*, evil spirits Natives believe inhabit the bones of the deceased.

A friend of mine decided these Indian mounds needed to be deactivated and hatched what he said was a Spirit-inspired strategy to rid the Sunshine State of the curses associated with developers building condos on Indian mounds or innocent children disturbing these sites, some of which are protected as historical grounds and others that haven't been marked. His notion was that retaliation arises when one disturbs an Indian mound and he wanted to put an end to this retaliation.

His strategy? He said the Lord showed him we should travel from one end of Florida to the other, visiting each of the Indian mounds in the state and worshiping there to disarm the ancient powers. He had a worship team and a caravan ready to go and he wanted me to join him on a five-day journey. My friend thought this would break a curse over the state of Florida. I did not go. I wanted no part of it. I did not feel this was my assignment, and others agreed his well-intended endeavor could open people up to warfare they didn't know how to fight. I declined the invitation. Ultimately, another man of God talked him out of launching the expedition and he didn't go either.

ARE INDIAN CURSES A MYTH?

Some believers don't believe in curses, despite clear evidence in the Bible. So it may be a stretch for them to believe in Indian curses. Is there such a thing? Or is this a movie-makers' myth? We know Native Americans issued curses in different places in America. I remember when I learned of the Seminole Indian curse on Florida. In fact, this is what prompted my friend to suggest we travel around Florida worshiping at Indian mounds to break the curse.

As the story goes, Florida Seminole Chief Osceola laid a curse on America during the Second Seminole War. Osceola was wooed to a meeting for peace talks in 1837. He went in good faith, but European-American settlers had no intention of having a peace talk. Instead, they captured him and he died in prison in 1838. President Fillmore recalled how Osceola's eyes, "seemed to blaze over as if in a trance. He swore that he would lay a curse on Florida, and that it would be the white man's graveyard forevermore, that giant rodents would rule the countryside, enslaving children into their magic kingdom, and that gore would forever stain the bushes of this land."[1] (Yes, Osceola used the words rats and magic kingdom, which reminds me of Disney World.)

Chief Osceola also put a curse of destruction on America, the U.S. government, and future presidents. One example is the curse of the year ending in zero. Seminoles released a curse that every president elected in a year ending in zero would die in office one way or another. Since 1840, history proved this to be true. U.S. presidents elected in a year ending in zero died, either through sickness or assassination. The first time that curse didn't land was with George W. Bush in 2000, leading some to believe the curse is broken.

Chroniclers say the Paugussetts, an Algonquian tribe that held large areas of land in Connecticut, were pushed off the island they called home. The Paugussetts cursed any building projects on the land back in 1614. Hundreds of years later, buildings don't survive on the island long. Nearby in Massachusetts, the Wampanoag tribe used a swamp they called Hockomock as an operational base. During the King Philipp's War, they cursed the colonists who stole their land. After that, colonists called it "Devil's Swamp" as the nature around the swamp failed to prosper.

In nearby Maine, the Sokokis Indians lived along the Saco River when British colonists started settling in the area in 1631. For a time, the colonists and the Natives lived in peace until sailors on an English ship decided to test the theory that Native American babies were born with the ability to swim. As one story goes, they threw a Sokoki baby into the water and it died. Squandro, one of the leaders, issued a curse in which the river's spirits would drown three white men a year until they departed the territory. For hundreds of years, no one would get in that river until the three-person quota was met. The *Main Sunday Telegram* reported in 1947 the curse was broken, as no one drowned in the river that year.

DANGERS IN ANCIENT INDIAN ARTIFACTS

It's not wisdom to stir up the demons that guard those Native American burial sites. News media has recounted horror stories about those who do. *The Biscayne Times* headlined a story, "The Curse of the Ancients."[2]

"The curse of the Miami Circle is unfolding before our eyes. The latest news is that Perez and his partners have been forced to return a majority of the $1 billion ICON Brickell complex to its lenders. Is it just another causality of the collapsed housing market? Or could there be deeper, ancestral forces at work?" *The Biscayne Times* reporter asked.

A friend of mine who owns a drilling and blasting business was contracted to do some work on a South Florida site where Indian mounds were present. He did not know they were Indian mounds and knew nothing about the spiritual dangers of proceeding with the job. What happened? His equipment broke down. He had it repaired and it broke down again. He purchased brand-new equipment, and it broke down. The losses were ongoing and beyond frustrating.

When this problem was brought to me, I remembered the Indian mound strategy. The Lord told me to ask him about the mounds, what they looked like, and how many there were. We discovered they were indeed Indian mounds. We prayed, but nothing deferred this curse. The equipment kept breaking, the job fell behind schedule, and frustration was rising. Finally, the crew had to abandon the job site.

Curses associated with Native American mounds, symbols, and jewelry are real. *The Guardian* reports, "Native American artifacts bring curse of suicides and FBI raids" and tells the harrowing story. The story began with three young boys decades ago scavenging for treasures in the desert in a small Utah town called Blanding. They would find centuries-old arrowheads, jewelry, ancient pots, and other artifacts. They considered it a treasure hunt.

But in 2010, 150 FBI agents arrested some of the citizens, including Jim Redd—one of the boys who dug in the desert—on charges of dealing in antiquities plundered from the state land. Redd committed suicide the next day. Two other defendants in the case also killed themselves in the months that followed. "It was a treasure hunt," Winston Hurst, one of the three boys, told *The Guardian*. "It was fun to trade with each other. That's what we did. We hunted rabbits, we dug in ruins. Who knew?"[3]

With that in mind, here is a list of Native American symbols and artifacts that can carry curses:

Dream Catchers

Dream catchers seem innocent and fun—and many Christians unknowingly display them in their homes, or even hang them over their children's beds. A dreamcatcher is essentially a beaded circle with a net that has feathers hanging from the bottom.

The dream catcher was birthed from a legend among the Ojibwe people. The legend says when you hang the contraption above your bed it will filter dreams. The good dreams, the legend says, will pass through to you, but the bad dreams will be captured in a web. But dream catchers do not catch evil spirits. Rather, like a Trojan horse, they bring evil spirits into your home.

Because prophetic people especially are fascinated with dreams and remembering dreams, dream catchers can be a tempting decoration that seems spiritual indeed. It's demonic. Dreamcatchers don't catch bad dreams, they invite demons into your home.

God's Eye

The God's Eye may look Christian, but it's also demonic in origin. A God's Eye is created by weaving a design out of yarn on a wooden cross. Typically, many colors are woven together to make it especially decorative. This is a popular craft for campers. This is a Native version of the all-seeing eye, which many believe carries powers to see and know things that we can't see with our naked eye. God's Eye comes from the Mexican Native American culture.

Thunderbird Jewelry and Pottery

Native American jewelry and pottery has an allure because of its unique decorative style, but the demons behind the beauty are not worth the trouble you could find if you wear these pieces or bring these symbols into your home. Native American culture considers the thunderbird a supernatural being of strength and power, controlling the upper world. By flapping its wings, the thunderbird throws lightning at the underworld creatures.

Totem Poles

Popular among First Nations tribes, totem poles are monumental carvings depicting symbols and figures. Keep in mind the word *totem* means "his kingship group" and the faces often represent dead ancestors, clan lineages, or mythical figures. Totem poles are often used to mark the remains of dead relatives. Totem poles may also depict insects, animals, fish, or plants. In some instances, totem poles are used to shame or ridicule people.

Squash Blossom Necklace

Squash blossoms are usually found in jewelry. Native Americans created a design that uses silver beads intermingled with other beads that take the shape of a bloom. At the bottom of the necklace is a pendant in the shape of a horseshoe called a Naja that looks somewhat like a quarter moon. This is where it goes wrong. Talisman created the Naja symbol, shaped like a womb, for protection. Only God is our protector.

Bear Tracks

The bear track symbolizes good omens and authority in Native American culture. It represents many things, such as protection, leadership, and strength. It is believed to help offer direction. Essentially it serves as a spirit helper or guide.

There are too many symbols to go into detail about each one. By now, you see there are demon spirits that work through these symbols, pottery, and jewelry. Here is a short list of additional symbols to watch out for in the context of Native American jewelry or art. Because this list is so extensive and the spirit guides so many, it's better to stay away from all Native American symbology. This is not a complete list.

- Bird tracks
- Broken arrows
- Broke cross
- Cactus
- Cedar wood masks represent owls
- Corn Plant
- Crows
- Cosmic cross
- Coyote
- Dancer
- Deer track
- Dragonfly
- Drums
- Feathers
- Hawks
- Hummingbirds
- Hogans (sweat houses)
- Kachina (a spiritual being)

- Knife wing
- Kokopelli
- Medicine wheel
- Morning star
- Rainbow man
- Rain cloud
- Ravens
- Spiders and spider webs
- Snakes
- Sun
- Turkeys
- Turtle
- Whirling logs
- Wolves
- Yei

NOTES

1. George Pendle, The Remarkable Millard Fillmore: The Unbelievable Life of a Forgotten President (New York, NY: Three Rivers Press, 2007), 84

2. Author Unknown, "The Curse of the Ancients," The Biscayne Times, n.d.; This article is no longer archived online.

3. Chris McGreal, "Native American artifacts bring curse of suicides and FBI raids," The Guardian, April 15, 2010, https://www.theguardian.com/world/2010/apr/15/blanding-treasure-hunt-suicides-fbi.

CHAPTER 5

UNCLEAN SPIRITS

COULD DEFILE YOUR HOME

When my daughter was about six years old, we were experiencing a lot of trouble in the house. I was not as experienced in spiritual warfare then as I am now, and I just could not get to the root of the issues. It seemed there was a force at work that I could not see with my eyes but could discern in the spirit. I kept praying.

One day, the Holy Spirit gave me a sudden revelation that startled me and compelled me to take immediate action. It was my daughter's bath time. Like most kids, she loved to play in the tub until her fingers and toes were all wrinkled up. She was playing with her toys and having a blast when the Holy Spirit illuminated the source of the issue. I looked in the bathtub and there were all manner of toys that took the form of what I now know to represent unclean spirits.

Shocked, I discreetly told my daughter bath time was over and bedtime was upon us. After I tucked her in safe and sound, I took every single one of those toys and got them out of the house. Of course, she was upset. She loved animals and could not understand why I would throw away some of her favorite toys. I'll admit, some of them seemed rather innocent on the surface, such as happy turtles.

None of these appeared grotesque any more than an angel of light appears evil. Paul warned us in Second Corinthians 11:14 that satan can appear as an angel of light. *The Message* says he is "dressing up as a beautiful angel of light." Other translations use the words *masquerades*, *disguises*, and *transforms*.

I tried as best I could to explain to her why they were not good toys. We went to the store that next day and I let her pick out whatever she wanted to replace those items, with the understanding that we could not have snakes, turtles, lizards, and other reptilian toys—even if they looked cute and wore smiles. Thank God, His grace was on it and we solved that issue.

WHAT ARE UNCLEAN SPIRITS?

Like angels, every demon that exists is not expressly named in the Bible. Only three angels—lucifer, Michael, and Gabriel—are named in Scripture, but we know there are millions upon millions of angels. Likewise, not every demon is named or classified in the Scripture. There are just too many.

Here's my point: when Scripture mentions a spirit by name it is worth special notation. The Bible clearly points to unclean spirits. The basic definition of an unclean spirit is something that defiles in thought and life. Technically, all spirits are unclean spirits from that perspective. But the Bible points to unclean spirits over and over again.

In fact, Scripture mentions unclean spirits over twenty times. The prophet Zechariah prophesied about a day when God will remove false prophets and unclean spirits from the land (see Zech. 13:2). Until then—until Christ's Second Coming—we will continue to see unclean spirits and other demon powers work to steal, kill, and destroy.

The first time we see unclean spirits mentioned in the New Testament is in conjunction with the believer's authority over them. When Jesus chose His twelve apostles, "He gave them power over unclean spirits, to cast them out, and to heal all kinds of sickness and all kinds of disease" (Matt. 10:1). Jesus Himself cast an unclean spirit out of a man in the synagogue, demonstrating that people who were seeking God could be demonized (see Mark 1:23).

People were amazed when they saw unclean spirits obey Jesus (see Mark 1:27). The unclean spirits themselves fell down before Him, crying out, "You are the Son of God" when they encountered Him (Mark 3:11). Even the man in the Gadarenes, who could not be bound with chains and was cutting himself with stones because of an unclean spirit, bowed to Jesus (see Mark 5:2). Unclean spirits will also bow to you, in Jesus' name, when you understand your authority. We'll talk more about your authority in a later chapter.

Revelation 16:13 gives us a dramatic account of an unclean spirit. John wrote, "And I saw three unclean spirits like frogs coming out of the mouth of the dragon, out of the mouth of the beast, and out of the mouth of the false prophet."

We are to have no fellowship with unclean spirits in our homes. In Second Corinthians 6:17-18, Paul wrote: "Come out from among them and be separate, says the Lord. Do not touch what is unclean, and I will receive you. I will be a Father to you, and you shall be My sons and daughters, says the Lord Almighty."

God has called us to be holy even as He is holy (see 1 Pet. 1:16). Unclean spirits work directly against that Holy Ghost agenda in our lives. Unclean spirits seek to steal, kill, and destroy by possessing people and tempting them to engage in sinful behavior. Unclean spirits pollute the souls of people and contaminate their relationship with the Lord. Unclean spirits can also be attached to things, waiting for an open door into someone's soul.

TYPES AND SHADOWS

In order to better understand unclean spirits on objects, we need to look at the Old Testament. Leviticus 11 gives a list of clean and unclean animals. Although we are not under Jewish dietary restrictions, many of the unclean animals represent unclean spirits. People say, well, why are they unclean if God created them?

That's a great question worthy of exploring because if you are not convinced that the animals I'm going to highlight represent unclean spirits and bringing them into your home can cause trouble, you won't get rid of them. Let's look at the theology behind this assertion in simple terms. It starts with the story of creation, particularly with the creation of living things in Genesis 1:20-25:

> *Then God said, "Let the waters abound with an abundance of living creatures, and let birds fly above the earth across the face of the firmament of the heavens." So God created great sea creatures and every living thing that moves, with which the waters abounded, according to their kind, and every winged bird according to its kind. And God saw that it was good. And God blessed them, saying, "Be fruitful and multiply, and fill the waters in the seas, and let birds multiply on the earth." So the evening and the morning were the fifth day.*
>
> *Then God said, "Let the earth bring forth the living creature according to its kind: cattle and creeping thing and beast of the earth, each according to its kind"; and it was so. And God made the beast of the earth according to its kind, cattle according to its kind, and everything that creeps on the earth according to its kind. And God saw that it was good.*

Everything God created was good. Let's take one step further back so we can move two steps forward. God created lucifer, but pride caused him to fall and transform into satan. God created the snakes, but satan possessed the snake and deceived Eve, then Adam, which resulted in the fall of man. The snake has been a symbol of evil ever since. All creation was impacted by the fall of man—not just mankind. After the fall of man, God first cursed the snake and then cursed the ground. It's important to note that God never cursed Adam.

Satan's corrupting influence not only touched mankind but many animals. Those animals, which are largely predators, are considered unclean. One day, God will redeem all creation. The Bible says the whole creation is groaning as in pains of childbirth (see Rom. 8:22). All of creation is waiting for redemption, when the lion and the lamb will lie down together during the millennial kingdom after Christ returns (see Isa. 11:6).

In the meantime, these symbols of animals deemed unclean in the Old Testament are the breeding ground for demon powers to infiltrate your home. Consider this list of unclean animals and other representations of evil spirits that could be in your home.

BEWARE REPTILIAN CREATURES

Reptilian creatures are worth special attention. The devil himself is depicted as a snake in the Garden of Eden (see Gen. 3). Leviathan in the Bible is reptilian (see Isa. 27:1). The Python spirit is mentioned in Acts 16. Throughout Scripture serpents are mentioned in the context of evil, including adders, vipers, and cobras. Proverbs speaks of how serpents bite and adders sting (see Prov. 23:32). These fall into the category of water spirits or marine demons. I write about these in my book *The Spiritual Warrior's Guide to Defeating Water Spirits*:

Battling marine demons is not your ordinary warfare. I believe the primary reason water spirits seem so powerful—even though they are actually no more powerful than any other demon and certainly nowhere near as powerful as the Spirit that raised Christ from the dead that dwells in you (see Romans 8:11)—I believe our ignorance has given marine demons what seems like an upper hand in battle.

...Marine demons have fallen below or failed to register on the radar screens of most of the church. We are ignorant of marine demons and therefore fail to discern their operations against our lives. Like a submarine with a radar reflector, marine demons divert attention to other demons so we can't see them.[1]

Remember, God sent frogs on the Egyptians as part of the plague in Exodus. Specifically, He smote the territory with frogs, saying:

> *So the river shall bring forth frogs abundantly, which shall go up and come into your house, into your bedroom, on your bed, into the houses of your servants, on your people, into your ovens, and into your kneading bowls. And the frogs shall come up on you, on your people, and on all your servants* (Exodus 8:3-4).

This was truly a plague. Frogs are unclean spirits. Kermit may be cute, but is it worth it?

Some reptilian creatures are rather obvious, like snakes and lizards. Others not so much. Some of these may even be pets in your home. Look for turtles and geckos too. Leviticus 11:29-31 warns:

> *These also shall be unclean to you among the creeping things that creep on the earth: the mole, the mouse, and the large lizard after its kind; the gecko, the monitor lizard, the sand reptile, the sand lizard, and the chameleon. These are unclean to you among all that creep.*

Beyond the reptiles actually named in the Bible, any reptilian creature should be avoided. These include alligators, crocodiles, skinks, iguanas, Komodo dragons, tuataras, Gila monsters, bearded dragons, boas, and the like. You may have some of these animals in aquariums and think they are harmless. But reptiles are often used in witchcraft. Consider the spells of witches that include "eye of newt, toe of frog, adder's fork, and lizard's leg" and you'll get a picture of how evildoers still rely on these symbols for their spells today. As for me and my house, we'll get some fish or birds instead.

INVESTIGATE INSECTS

Insects can represent evil spirits. God told the Israelites winged insects that go on all fours are detestable (see Lev. 11:20). Not all insects are banned. The Bible points to ants as wise (see Prov. 6:6).

Commentators suggest the Bible is speaking of insects that not only fly but also creep in a horizontal position, close to the ground (not specifically to how many legs they have). This would include flies, which are seen in the plague on Egypt. Bees, hornets, beetles, and mosquitos also fly and creep. God used hornets to drive out Israel's enemies (see Exod. 23:28), and He used gnats as part of the ten plagues against Egypt (see Exod. 8:16).

Insects are popular in home décor, and party supply stores sell bug-themed plates, napkins, banners, and the like. HGTV.com even offers a list of "Our 10 Fave Stylish (Not Creepy) Insect Décor" because "insect decor is a now thing."[2] That list includes an insect tapestry headboard that looks pretty creepy to me and salad plates depicting black and white bugs on white ceramic. Again, creepy. See how the devil creeps in?

ARACHNIDS RISING

Arachnids are a class of animals that includes spiders, mites, ticks, and daddy longlegs. Although spiders do have some positive connotations in Scripture, in pop culture the evil side of spiders is typically demonstrated. Spiders relate to witchcraft. Job 8:14 compares the trust of the hypocrite to the spider's web or house. Isaiah 59:5 speaks of how the wicked weave a spider's web.

Yet we sing "Itsy Bitsy Spider" to our children and read stories about Little Miss Muffet. Maybe you remember: "Little Miss Muffet sat on a tuffet, eating her curds and whey; there came a big spider, who sat down beside her and frightened Miss Muffet away." We shouldn't be scared of spiders, but we shouldn't celebrate them either.

SERIOUS ABOUT SCORPIONS

There's no mistaking the scorpion's sting. The symptoms range from tingling and burning all the way to difficulty swallowing and breathing, blurry vision, and seizures. Revelation 9:5 speaks of the scorpion's torment. God will use scorpions in the end times as a means of judgment.

God gave us authority over scorpions and what they symbolize, meaning they must be evil. In Luke 10:19 Jesus said, "Behold, I give you the authority to trample on serpents and scorpions, and over all the power of the enemy, and nothing shall by any means hurt you." God wouldn't give us authority over something that wasn't harmful to us.

THE DANGER OF DRAGONS

There are no real life dragons today, but the Bible does mention dragons—and it's not in a positive context. The dragon is a symbol of satan himself. Revelation 12:9 reads, "So the great dragon was cast out, that serpent of old, called the Devil and Satan, who deceives the whole world; he was cast to the earth, and his angels were cast out with him." In Revelation 20, the dragon is seized and thrown into the pit for one thousand years. Leviathan is sometimes mentioned as a dragon in Scripture (see Isa. 27:1).

In China, the dragon is reverenced for its dignity and powers for good. But this is another example of satan disguising himself as an angel of light. When I was in Hong Kong and Taiwan, there were dragons everywhere. People love to give us gifts when we travel, but I am not bringing a dragon or a silk robe with dragons back into my home.

WICKED BIRDS OF THE SKY

Certain birds like vultures, ravens, falcons, osprey, gulls, herons, bats, hoopoes, hawks, and owls are representative of evil spirits. In Leviticus 11:13-19 God told the Israelites:

> *And these you shall regard as an abomination among the birds;*
> *they shall not be eaten, they are an abomination: the eagle, the*
> *vulture, the buzzard, the kite, and the falcon after its kind;*
> *every raven after its kind, the ostrich, the short-eared owl, the*

sea gull, and the hawk after its kind; the little owl, the fisher owl, and the screech owl; the white owl, the jackdaw, and the carrion vulture; the stork, the heron after its kind, the hoopoe, and the bat.

Some prophetic people like owls, but owls are symbolic of unclean animals and symbols of predators. Symbolically, they are used to picture desolation, judgment, mourning, and deep loneliness. The prophets Isaiah and Zephaniah did not have owl mugs or T-shirts. They wrote of owls residing in wastelands. Consider Isaiah 34:8-11:

For it is the day of the Lord's vengeance, the year of recompense for the cause of Zion. Its streams shall be turned into pitch, and its dust into brimstone; its land shall become burning pitch. It shall not be quenched night or day; its smoke shall ascend forever. From generation to generation it shall lie waste; no one shall pass through it forever and ever. But the pelican and the porcupine shall possess it, also the owl and the raven shall dwell in it. And He shall stretch out over it the line of confusion and the stones of emptiness.

There are three other Scriptures that will drive this home and perhaps convince you to get wicked birds of the sky out of your home. Isaiah 13:21 reads, "But wild beasts of the desert will lie there, and their houses will be full of owls; ostriches will dwell there, and wild goats will caper there." Psalm 102:3-6 reads:

For my days are consumed like smoke, and my bones are burned like a hearth. My heart is stricken and withered like grass, so that I forget to eat my bread. Because of the sound of my groaning my bones cling to my skin. I am like a pelican of the wilderness; I am like an owl of the desert.

And Zephaniah 2:13-14 tells us:

And He will stretch out His hand against the north, destroy Assyria, and make Nineveh a desolation, as dry as the wilderness. The herds shall lie down in her midst, every beast of the nation. Both the pelican and the bittern shall lodge on the capitals of her pillars; their voice shall sing in the windows; desolation shall be at the threshold; for He will lay bare the cedar work.

WOLVES, RATS, JACKALS, AND OTHER ANIMALS

Besides the dragon and the snake, the wolf is a symbol of the devil and those who serve him. John 10:12 says, "But a hireling, he who is not the shepherd, one who does not own the sheep, sees the wolf coming and leaves the sheep and flees; and the wolf catches the sheep and scatters them." Jesus also points to false prophets as wolves in sheep's clothing—there is danger (see Matt. 7:15).

Rats, hyenas, cankerworms, foxes, hedgehogs, and jackals are representatives of evil. In his distress, Job called himself a "brother of jackals and a companion of owls" (Job 30:29 MEV). Psalm 44:19 speaks of being crushed in the place of jackal and covered with the shadow of death, while Psalm 63:10 speaks to those who fall by the sword being a portion for jackals.

The habitation of jackals is mentioned several times and it's not a place you want to live. It speaks of desert places and destruction.

OCEAN CREATURES AND MARINE DEMONS

I wrote an entire book on marine demons, which are also called water spirits. Again, it's called *The Spiritual Warrior's Guide to Defeating Water Spirits*. Not all creatures in the water represent evil, but many do. Beyond pythons and crocodiles (representative of Leviathan), squid, octopi, mermaids (representative of Dagon, a false god), and hippopotami are a few water creatures that represent evil in the Bible.

Marine demons are especially stealthy. First Peter 5:8 reveals the enemy roams about like a lion in fierce hunger looking for someone to devour. Usually, you can hear the enemy roar through the voice of fear or some other vain imagination before he gets close enough to devour. Marine demons roam undetected, making as little sound as possible until they are close enough to strike.

If you have items including pictures, T-shirts, media, and so on that depict unclean spirits, it's time to deal with them and the curse that could be lurking behind them.

NOTES

1. Jennifer LeClaire, *The Spiritual Warrior's Guide to Defeating Water Spirits* (Shippensburg, PA: Destiny Image Publishers, 2018).

2. Erica Reitman, "Our 10 Fave Stylish (Not Creepy) Insect Décor," HGTV.com, May 21, 2018, https://www.hgtv.com/design/packages/shopping/shop-like-a-pro/insect-decor-is-now-a-thing.

CHAPTER 6

THE ALL SEEING EYE

MAY BE WATCHING YOU

N ew Age has creeped into Christianity. According to Pew Research analysis, many Christians hold New Age beliefs, including reincarnation, astrology, psychics, and the presence of spiritual energy in physical objects like mountains or trees.

While eighty percent of Christians say they believe in God as described in the Bible, sixty percent believe in one or more of the four New Age beliefs listed above, ranging from 47 percent of evangelical Protestants to roughly seven in ten Catholics and Protestants in the historically black tradition, according to the study.[1]

The New Age movement includes a cadre of spiritual beliefs and practices that deal with "mind, body, spirit." The movement is eclectic and pulls from esoteric traditions such as Spiritualism, New Thought, and Theosophy. Common beliefs in the New Age movement include a belief in the universe as a power, pantheism (God is in everything), our minds create our reality, and our own experience is our truth.

New Agers do not believe our problem is sin, but that we need to find our "higher consciousness" through breathing, diet, crystals, yoga, spirit guides, and meditation. New Agers do not deny the existence of Christ and even appreciate His teachings. New Agers can, in many ways, sound like Christians in their quest for love and peace. But they do not see Jesus as the only way to the Father, the way, the truth, and the life (see John 14:6).

SELLING SYNCRETISM

New Agers, as well as some other religions, practice syncretism. Syncretism is a blend of different religions, cultures, or schools of thought. Syncretism defies logic, often mixing contradictory beliefs in the name of unity.

The New Age movement is syncretistic, blending various religions, relying on various gods, and crediting the "universe" with power it doesn't have. Chrislam, as its name suggests, is also syncretistic, blending elements of Christianity and Islam. Muslims use Chrislam theology as a way into Christian pulpits, essentially opening the door to false worship.

How does God feel about syncretism? "For you shall worship no other god, for the Lord, whose name is Jealous, is a jealous God" (Exod. 34:14). Jesus said, "If you love Me, keep My commandments" (John 14:15, and, "'You shall love the Lord your God with all your heart, with all your soul, with all your strength, and with all your mind,' and 'your neighbor as yourself'" (Luke 10:27). Jesus said, "He who is not with Me is against Me, and he who does not gather with Me scatters abroad" (Matt. 12:30).

Although I am not opposed to people from different faiths working together for the common good, many times such endeavors lead to Christians compromising their beliefs in the name of unity—and that's one of the key dangers of syncretism. We cannot compromise the Word of God for the sake of getting along with Muslims, Buddhists, Hindus, Mormons, or anyone else. Once we've started embracing elements of other religions, we've compromised the gospel that has the power to save those who know Christ in name only.

Don't be fooled. Just because something has Christian elements doesn't make it Christian. In his letter to the church at Philippi, Paul points to "enemies of the cross" (Phil. 3:18). Islam is not a friend of the cross. Buddha was not a friend of the cross. Leaders of false religions are not friends of the cross. And we cannot reconcile the enemies of the cross to the Christ who hung upon a tree to pay the price for their sin if we compromise the gospel and essentially worship their god.

IS NEW AGE SYMBOLOGY IN YOUR HOUSE?

Many symbols New Agers use were around before the New Age movement began, and you may have some of them in your house. Some of these symbols even look Christian, but there's a deeper meaning behind these objects and practices that you may not understand. Here is a short list of common New Age objects and practices that can defile your home. Again, this is not a complete list.

Third Eye

Also called the mind's eye or inner eye, the third eye is usually depicted on the forehead of a statue. It's gives one extraordinary sight and leads you into higher consciousness. New Agers see it as a symbol of spiritual enlightenment that opens them up to impactful mental images. God is the giver of true visions and dreams, but the third eye can open you up to false dreams and visions.

The Yin-Yang

Rooted in ancient Chinese philosophy, yin-yang represents the concept of dualism, a doctrine that the universe is under the dominion of two opposing principles—good and evil. It literally means "dark-bright" or "negative-positive." It's usually depicted as a circle divided in two with a curvy line running through the middle.

Peace Sign

This is hard for many to accept, because Jesus is the Prince of Peace. Historians will tell you it was created during Britain's campaign for nuclear disarmament. But the roots actually go deeper. But if you dig below the surface, you'll discover this is the cross of Nero, the Roman emperor who hated Christianity. The broken-armed, upside-down cross represents Christian persecution.

The Ankh

The ankh sort of looks like a cross, but it dons an oval loop at the top of the vertical bar. It is an ancient Egyptian hieroglyphic symbol for life. New Agers started wearing jewelry that displays the ankh during the 1960s.

Unicorn Horn

Unicorns are in the Bible. Job 39 speaks of a unicorn whose strength is great and Psalm 29:6 describes unicorns skipping like calves. Isaiah 34:7 talks about unicorns traveling like bullocks and bleeding when they die (KJV). Unicorns are a biblical symbol of strength. But wearing unicorn horns does not glorify God. Also called alicorns, the New Age movement purports unicorns to be symbols of imaginary creatures that carry healing powers and purification properties. All healing power comes from God, not a unicorn.

Astrology

Astrology is a form of divination that supposes the stars and planets influence our lives based on their position in the sky. People may ask you, "What's your sign?" This is New Age talk that is based on the zodiac, such as Aries, Taurus, Gemini, or Leo. The horoscope is based on astrology and uses your "sign" to tell you what is going to happen in your life on any given day or season. You can usually find horoscopes in newspapers near the comics section.

Crystals, Stones, and Gems

Crystals, stones, and gems are not entirely evil. God created them. But New Agers put their faith in crystals, stones, and gems. New Agers believe these crystals, stones, and gems carry spiritual powers, including healing. The amethyst, some believe, can fight off hangovers. Some gemstone-infused oils work, they believe, to stimulate heart chakras while simultaneously fighting acne. Again, God is the only one who brings true supernatural healing.

Burning Incense

Burning incense of herbs is seen as a way to clean your home of bad energy, but it's also used in idol worship. Incense attracts demons rather than driving them out. Burning incense opens the door for curses, not blessings. Incense was part of the burial process in ancient Egypt.

Self-Help Books for Enlightenment

Many self-help books in your home may contain New Age principles and practices. There is nothing wrong with self-help books in general, but if the teachers aren't rooted in Christian thinking and if their principles aren't found in the pages of the Bible, they can open you and your home up to evil influences.

Pegasus

Pegasus is a mythical winged horse, typically pure white. Pegasus is seen in the New Age movement as representing speed, strength, and artistic inspiration. New World Encyclopedia reports, "Encompassing beauty and a sense of majesty, it is a guide for humankind beyond the physical world to the realm where the spirit can soar without limit."[2]

A Rainbow in the Heart

Although the rainbow is a sign of God's covenant with man never to flood the earth again, New Agers, like other special interest groups, believe every person must have a rainbow in their heart to lead you to your higher self.

These are just a few of the many symbols. Others include the Sun god, a triangle with three overlapping circles, a crescent moon representing the Queen of Heaven, the Egyptian holy bug, crystal balls, pyramids representing eternity, and spirals. Meanwhile, practices like yoga— which means "to yoke"—offer poses to over 330 million Hindu gods. Some call it the missionary arm of the New Age movement. There is no such thing as Christian yoga, which aims to manipulate your life force energy through breathing exercises. God is our breath and our life. If you have representations of these symbols in your home, you must cleanse your home from this evil.

NOTES

1. Claire Gecewicz, "'New Age' beliefs common among both religious and nonreligious Americans," Pew Research, October 1, 2018, https://www.pewresearch.org/fact-tank/2018/10/01/new-age-beliefs-common-among-both-religious-and-nonreligious-americans.

2. New World Encyclopedia, "Pegasus," https://www.newworldencyclopedia.org/entry/Pegasus.

CHAPTER 7

VIOLENT MEDIA

CAN UNLEASH DEMONS

W hen I was in high school, one of my best friends, we'll call her Mattie, started dating a guy who was a little bit older—and a lot of trouble. His hobbies were drugs and witchcraft. I knew he was bad news, but my friend was enamored with his charisma and good looks.

Soon, Mattie started coming to school looking exhausted. It turns out she was staying up until the wee hours of the morning reading a book he gave her. (I can't remember the name of it but it was about secrets of the dead and witchcraft.)

When Mattie's mother found the wicked manuscript, she insisted the book go into the trash. Mattie lied and told her mother the book was destroyed but continued to stay up at night reading it in her dark bedroom with a flashlight. She was fascinated with its contents, as these wicked spirts seduced her.

Then it happened. The spirits she invited into her home through this fascination with the book started wreaking havoc on the house. Things in her room would rattle and she heard the sound of blowing wind and ominous voices. This, of course, frightened her into insomnia. Soon enough, Mattie had an absolute meltdown in anatomy lab in front of the entire class. When she got rid of the book, she returned to normal.

THE SPIRIT OF VIOLENCE

Violent media—from books and magazines to television and movies to video games and music—can unleash demons in your home. Essentially, when you bring violent media into your home—or any form of inappropriate media, including pornography or materials with foul language—you are opening the front door to demons.

A spirit of violence is raging in the earth, and it doesn't take prophetic insight to see it. The World Health Organization reports hundreds of thousands of homicides every year, and nearly one-fourth of adults report being a victim of physical abuse as children. That's just the tip of the iceberg. Although we do see violence in the pages of the Bible, it was violence against the enemy. God has always condemned violence against the innocent.

Psalm 11:5 assures, "The Lord tests the righteous, but the wicked and the one who loves violence His soul hates." That's a strong statement that makes it crystal clear that God hates violence. If you need more, Proverbs

3:31 admonishes us, "Do not envy a man of violence and do not choose any of his ways" (ESV). Remember, violence was one of the reasons God flooded the earth in the days of Noah. Genesis 6:11-14 reads:

> *The earth also was corrupt before God, and the earth was filled with violence. So God looked upon the earth, and indeed it was corrupt; for all flesh had corrupted their way on the earth. And God said to Noah, "The end of all flesh has come before Me, for the earth is filled with violence through them; and behold, I will destroy them with the earth. Make yourself an ark of gopherwood; make rooms in the ark, and cover it inside and outside with pitch."*

You know the rest of the story. God hates violence, so we should not consume violent media in any venue. But when we bring it into our home we are agreeing with the ways of violence. We should not be entertained by something God hates; rather, we should hate what God hates. Indeed, Proverbs 6 lists hands that shed innocent blood as an abomination.

VIOLENT STATISTICS

The American Academy of Family Physicians (AAFP) offers a cadre of statistics on violent media and its impacts. "An average American youth will witness 200,000 violent acts on television before age 18. ...Studies analyzing the content of popular cartoons noted that they contain 20 to 25 violent acts per hour, which is about five times as many as prime time programs."[1]

Many games have violent content, and studies have shown a significant association between violent content and increases in aggression, desensitization to violence, decreases in positive social behaviors, and increases in delinquent behaviors. Content analysis has shown that in music videos more than 80 percent of violence is perpetrated by attractive people, and that it depicts acts of violence mainly against women and minorities.

Studies have found that 91 percent of movies on television contained violence, even extreme violence. Multiple studies have shown a strong association, and suspicion or suggestion of causality, between exposure to violence in the media and aggressive or violent behavior in viewers. These are just some of the statistics the AAFP gathered. The studies are ongoing and the findings are troublesome.

In our era, we've witnessed the rise of social media. That has made it easy for people to share violence with a few keystrokes. In fact, social media is so pervasive and makes it so easy to share violent content that two Wisconsin preteens lured a friend into the woods and knifed her 19 times.[2] When police investigated why they did it, they responded "Slenderman" made them do it. Slenderman is a fictional character found in an Internet meme that promotes violence. That wasn't the only act of violence linked to Slenderman.

VIOLENT MEDIA TO WATCH FOR

Violence isn't too difficult to pick up on, but if you aren't aware of some of the latest trends you could miss it. Even seemingly innocent pop music contains quite a lot of violence. When I got born again, I threw away thousands of dollars' worth of CDs—and I didn't even know the principle I am teaching in this book. I had the conviction of the Holy Spirit. I have only listened to Christian music in my home.

Before you bring media into your house—or air it in your home—look at the ratings, read the descriptions, and look at the reviews. Sites like Movieguide.org offer a Christian perspective on media as it comes out. Some of your choices should be common sense—and you may never willfully bring violent media or watch it in your home. But if you live with other people, you could be subject to the spiritual warfare through what others bring in.

For all the statistics that demonstrate the harmful impacts of violent media on children, know that it's beyond psychological impacts to the demon power we open ourselves up to when we find an adrenaline rush, a thrill, or are otherwise entertained through media that glorifies violence. While some movies about wars show violence, this is different from glorifying violence. Be watchful.

NOTES

1. "Violence in the Media and Entertainment (Position Paper)," American Academy of Family Physicians, accessed March 20, 2021, https://www.aafp.org/about/policies/all/violence-media .html.

2. Meredith E. Gansner, MD, "'The Internet Made Me Do It'—Social Media and Potential for Violence in Adolescents," *Psychiatric Times,* Vol 34 No 9, Volume 34, Issue 9, September 5, 2017, https://www.psychiatrictimes.com/view/-internet-made -me-do-itsocial-media-and-potential-violence-adolescents.

CHAPTER 8

MEDIUMISTIC
AND SATANIC OBJECTS

was excited about going to New Zealand. We were doing a three-city teaching tour, including Christchurch, Auckland, and Wellington. Our first stop, unfortunately, was Wellington. I say unfortunately because New Zealand is a beautiful nation and my first experience there was not so beautiful.

Sitting at the southern end of the North Island, Wellington is known to many as "the coolest little capital in the world." That may be true, but we were staying on Witchcraft Row.

Of course, it's not officially called Witchcraft Row, but that's my name for it. We stayed in the beach area where a strip of stores lined either side of the street, sort of like Duvall Street in Key West. Every few stores was a witchcraft peddler, a pornographic store, a tattoo shop with wicked imagery, and a pizza shop called Hell Pizza: Home of the Seven Deadly Sins. Occult shops were left and right and everywhere in between.

I have never been in city with such a heavy concentration of witchcraft. It was startling. I remember being exhausted the entire time with burning eyes and just feeling like something was dreadfully wrong. The witchcraft was affecting us and we were also feeling the Lord's grief. Unfortunately, we were sort of trapped there until our host took us to the next city. Needless to say, we spent most of our time there praying against the witchcraft.

A REVIVAL OF THE DEVIL'S WITCHCRAFT

Watching old videos of healing evangelists like Kathryn Kuhlman, A.A. Allen, Jack Coe, and Oral Roberts is one of my favorite things to do. I've consumed hundreds of hours of videos showing the miracle-working power of God and bold revival preaching that makes no apologies for the Rock of Offense.

While watching an A.A. Allen miracle reel my ears perked up when I heard the late Brother Allen declare a revival of the devil's witchcraft. Of course, this was back in the 1950s. What was a revival of witchcraft then has turned into a full-blown movement.

"An awful lot of people are sick, diseased, and afflicted under a curse, under a spell because of the present revival of witchcraft around the world," Allen declared. "There has never been a time in history when there has been such a devil's revival of witchcraft."

Think about it for a minute. In Allen's day, there was no such thing as Harry Potter. Allen made this declaration before popular TV shows like *Bewitched*, *Charmed*, and *The Witches of East End*—and before films like

Rosemary's Baby, The Blair Witch Project, and *Season of the Witch.* Indeed, it was before children's media like *Meg and Mog, The Witch Family,* and *Witches in Stitches* hit the mainstream.

In recent years, we've seen the devil pressing hard to bring witchcraft deeper into our schools, our homes, and our entertainment venues. While editor of Charisma magazine, we reported on how a witchcraft-inspired challenge is luring kids into summoning demons. It's called Charlie Charlie and it's sweeping the nation and the world under the guise of a carefree fortune-telling game. Faith leaders are sounding the alarm.

I'm believing for a Third Great Awakening. But the devil is clearly driving toward a great awakening of the occult. This revival of the devil's witchcraft is unto an awakening to the occult that will set the very elect up to be deceived, it if is possible (see Matt. 24:24). False signs and wonders will rise, along with false prophets and false christs.

WITCHCRAFT IS EN VOGUE

This is no surprise. Since the 1990s, witchcraft and pagan practices have risen rapidly. In 2019, *The New York Times* published an article entitled, "When Did Everybody Become a Witch?" With 1.5 million potential practicing witches across the U.S., witchcraft has more followers than the 1.4 million mainline members of the Presbyterian church, according to a 2014 Pew Research Center survey.

The psychic services industry, including astrology, aura reading, mediumship, tarot-card reading, and palmistry, is now worth $2 billion annually, according to industry analysis firm IBIS World. That number is expected to grow. I believe all the witchcraft movies, television shows, and books like the Harry Potter series have helped contribute to the rise.

What's most troubling is the rise of so-called "Christian witches." Christian witches—witches who claim to serve the Lord Jesus Christ— have emerged with a vengeance. Some of them are targeting politicians and churches. There is no such thing as a Christian witch, but many well-meaning Christians are practicing witchcraft because they don't understand the Word of God. I write more about Christian witches in my book *Discerning Prophetic Witchcraft*.

GOD HATES WITCHCRAFT

If you are reading this book, you probably understand this but let me say it anyway: God hates witchcraft and everything to do with witchcraft. Scripture after Scripture makes this clear. Let's look at a few that demonstrate God's hatred for every form of witchcraft.

> *Give no regard to mediums and familiar spirits; do not seek after them, to be defiled by them: I am the Lord your God* (Leviticus 19:31).

> *And the person who turns to mediums and familiar spirits, to prostitute himself with them, I will set My face against that person and cut him off from his people* (Leviticus 20:6).

> *You shall not eat anything with the blood, nor shall you practice divination or soothsaying* (Leviticus 19:26).

And when they say to you, "Seek those who are mediums and wizards, who whisper and mutter," should not a people seek their God? Should they seek the dead on behalf of the living? To the law and to the testimony! If they do not speak according to this word, it is because there is no light in them (Isaiah 8:19-20).

So Saul died for his unfaithfulness which he had committed against the Lord, because he did not keep the word of the Lord, and also because he consulted a medium for guidance. But he did not inquire of the Lord, therefore He killed him, and turned the kingdom over to David the son of Jesse (1 Chronicles 10:13-14).

Exodus 22:18 goes so far as to say, "You shall not permit a sorceress to live." Yes, death was the penalty for witchcraft under Mosaic law. Of course, God loves witches and is giving them time to repent in the new covenant. But He still hates witchcraft. Have you ever wondered why?

God hates witchcraft because it counterfeits the power of God and brings us into the domain of satan. Witchcraft is in the realm of idolatry, and demonstrates a reliance on a spirit other than the Holy Spirit to lead us and guide us or to move on our behalf. The Bible says the Holy Spirit will show us things to come, but when we turn to mediums, psychics, and the like we are insulting His grace and denying His truth-giving power.

COMMON WITCHCRAFT SYMBOLS

Witchcraft can creep into your home through symbols you don't recognize, so if it looks odd or feels wrong, throw it out. Decorative journals and boxes, jewelry, T-shirts, even labels on canned goods can carry witchcraft symbols. Here is a list of what to watch out for, but remember it's not always so obvious. (Again, this is not an exhaustive list, but if you find these types of things in your home, it's time for a cleanse.)

- Zodiacs
- Ouija boards
- Tarot cards
- Automatic writing
- Psychic books
- Ritualistic cups
- Sacred salts
- Burning sage
- Statues
- Amulets and charms
- Greenman box
- Voodoo dolls and pins
- Baby dolls
- Witchcraft books
- Spell books
- Peace sign upside down

- Witching sticks

- Crystal balls

There are also occult witchcraft symbols that are hidden in logos of companies. One example is the winged sun-disk symbol. Chrysler, Aston Martin, Bentley, Mini, and Harley Davidson use this symbol in their logos. The ancient Egyptian symbol also represents groups like the Rosicrucians and the Freemasons.

Meanwhile, Gucci, Chanel, and DC Shoes—as well as the MasterCard logo—use a symbol that resembles the *vesica piscis*, which appear as two overlapping circles with a fish in the middle. Many point to its origins as representing the vulva of the goddess. The list goes on and on. We don't want to be religious, but we also don't want to be ignorant. This is why we need the Holy Spirit's leadership.

CHAPTER 9

LUCKY
CHARMS

When I was growing up, I had a rabbit's foot. It was supposed to bring me good luck. We thought our lucky pencil would help us win the test, our lucky shirt would put forth a good impression, and so on and so on and so on. As Christians, we understand there is no such thing as luck. We don't walk in luck, we walk in the favor of God.

If we step on a crack, we won't break our mother's back. We aren't cursed with seven years of back luck if we break a mirror. Friday the 13th doesn't spook us. And we aren't concerned about walking under a ladder or when a black cat crosses our path. Beginner's luck is a fantasy, and I know from experience that if I find a penny and pick it up, all day long I won't have good luck.

Bad luck doesn't really come in threes. Pulling a wishbone won't make my dreams come true. Knocking on wood won't ward off evil.

Crossing my fingers won't change my circumstances. The list of superstitions—some sillier than others—goes on and on. Most of us don't believe these old wives' tales, but we may still have symbols of them in our homes.

ROLLING THE DICE

Proverbs 16:33 tells us, "We may toss the coin and roll the dice, but God's will is greater than luck" (TPT). If you want to use the world's terms, when you adopt lucky charms or objects you're rolling the dice on demonic oppression. Put another way, you are playing with fire—strange fire to put it in biblical terms. And you know what happens with you play with fire. (You get burned.)

Luck is an idol. Superstition is idolatry. Good luck charms, then, are essentially mini idols that you are treating like a god who can bring about your hopes and dreams. But there are even religious superstitions and good luck charms, like necklaces with saints depicted on them for protection.

Paul told Timothy, "Be quick to abstain from senseless traditions and legends, but instead be engaged in the training of truth that brings righteousness" (1 Tim. 4:7 TPT). *The Message* puts it this way, "Stay clear of silly stories that get dressed up as religion." The Amplified Bible, Classic Edition says, "But refuse and avoid irreverent legends (profane and impure and godless fictions, mere grandmothers' tales) and silly myths, and express your disapproval of them."

ALL GOOD THINGS COME FROM GOD

James, the apostle of practical faith, said it well, "Every good gift and every perfect gift is from above, and comes down from the Father of lights" (James 1:17). *The Passion Translation* puts it this way: "Every gift God freely gives us is good and perfect, streaming down from the Father of lights, who shines from the heavens with no hidden shadow or darkness and is never subject to change."

The Bible says our God is in the heavens and does all He pleases. The Bible says when we're obedient, blessings will chase us down and overtake us (see Deut. 28:2). You don't need a lucky charm. Obedience will bring a blessing on your city, your country, the fruit of your body, and so on and so on and so on. Everything you put your hand to will prosper. It's not the least bit ironic that when you rely on lucky charms and objects, the exact opposite happens sooner or later.

Deuteronomy 28:15 tells us, "But it shall come to pass, if you do not obey the voice of the Lord your God, to observe carefully all His commandments and His statutes which I command you today, that all these curses will come upon you and overtake you." It's not that God is cursing you, but you have opened the door for a curse. The curse has a right to land and often does.

Consider this list of lucky charms, objects, and symbols that you may find in your house or car. This is not the end-all list but gives you a good start of the likely objects you may find in your midst.

- Rabbit's foot
- Four-leaf clovers

- Lucky horseshoe charms
- Fuzzy dice
- Ladybug charms
- Lucky number charms
- Rainbow good luck charms
- Lucky pennies
- Acorns as lucky charms
- Patron saints necklaces
- Wish-makers, such as stray eyelashes, wishing wells
- Cat's eye

Different cultures have good luck charms and superstitions that are odd. You may receive one as a gift. If so, don't keep it. For example:

- In England, acorns are thought to protect one's health.
- In Sweden, the Dala horse—also called the Dalecarlian horse—is a carved figure of a horse that was considered holy in ancient times and is now a symbol of good luck.
- In Turkey, the nazar represents the evil eye. It's an amulet for protection against wicked people.
- In Poland, Slovakia, and the Czech Republic, carp scales eaten at Christmas give you good luck all year long.
- In China, the feng shui charm or Golden Toad symbolizes both luck and success.
- In Ghana, gris-gris—voodoo amulets—are used to ward off evil spirts and keep good luck.

- In America, eating pork, rice, and black-eyed peas is supposed to make you wise and prosperous.

- In Ukraine, highly decorated Easter eggs represent love, health, wealth, and fertility.

- In Japan, the Maneki-neko with a paw that waves is believed to attract customers to a business.

- In Israel and other Middle Eastern countries, the hamsa—a palm-shaped amulet—thought to bring good luck.

- In Italy, the cornicello, which means lucky horn, purports to ward off the evil eye.

- In India and Thailand, elephants are a common symbol of good luck.

- In France, yarn dolls called Nanette and Rintintin are used as good luck charms.

- In Brazil, Peru, and Italy the Mano Figa, a thumb that sticks up between the pointer and middle finger, calls on the goddess of fertility.

- In Germany, they have luck pigs often pictured on cards around New Year.

- In Mexico, milagros—the Spanish word for miracles—are religious charms that may look like animals, angels, or crosses. They are carried in a pocket for good luck.

- In Guatemala you'll find worry dolls, which are believed to help you fall asleep.

The list goes on and on. Before you bring home that souvenir, make sure it doesn't have a demon or a curse attached to it. Check the history of the items you are buying.

CHAPTER 10

FALSE
RELIGIOUS SYMBOLS

n my parents' house, they displayed a Buddha on the shelf. He was burgundy with a big smile and an even bigger belly. My dad told me if I rubbed his belly, I would have good luck. I remember trying it and being as disappointed as I was when I made wish and threw a penny in the fountain at the mall. I had a disdain for Buddha and his empty promises.

Several years ago, as part of an exercise routine, I walked up eleven flights of stairs from the ground up, crossing through the hallways on my way to the staircase on the other side. I did this habitually when I went downstairs to get the mail. Every day on the seventh floor, I would pass a doorway in the hall guarded by a Buddha statue. I felt like it was staring me down and wanted to throw it down the trash chute.

Every day when I walked by that Buddha I broke the powers of witchcraft and commanded it to be removed. After a few weeks, the

Buddha suddenly disappeared. I never saw it again. No, I did not throw it down the trash chute. I don't know what happened to it. It sort of reminded me of the demise of Dagon, the Philistine god. First Samuel 5:3-5 demonstrates how false gods cannot stand against Jehovah:

> *When the Ashdodites arose early the next morning, behold, Dagon had fallen on his face to the ground before the ark of the Lord. So they took Dagon and set him in his place again. But when they arose early the next morning, behold, Dagon had fallen on his face to the ground before the ark of the Lord. And the head of Dagon and both the palms of his hands were cut off on the threshold; only the trunk of Dagon was left to him. Therefore neither the priests of Dagon nor all who enter Dagon's house tread on the threshold of Dagon in Ashdod to this day* (NASB).

THE DANGER OF FALSE RELIGIOUS SYMBOLS

From Dagon to Buddha to beyond, the symbols of false religions are dangerous to keep company with. Symbols of false religions can carry demons or curses that pollute your home. That's because they are essentially icons of evil. In Exodus 20:3, the Lord said, "You shall have no other gods before Me." He doesn't even want the other gods beside Him. Isaiah 43:10 makes it clear, "Besides me there is no other god" (GNT). And Jesus put it this way—you can only serve one master (see Matt. 6:24).

False religious symbols are typically representing false gods. Jehovah doesn't even want us to make mention of other gods (see Exod. 23:13).

There is no salvation in other gods (see Acts 4:12). Rather, there is deception. People rely on these false gods, these idols, for protection, healing, and more. But Psalm 115:4-8 makes it clear:

Their idols are silver and gold, the work of men's hands. They have mouths, but they do not speak; eyes they have, but they do not see; they have ears, but they do not hear; noses they have, but they do not smell; they have hands, but they do not handle; feet they have, but they do not walk; nor do they mutter through their throat. Those who make them are like them; so is everyone who trusts in them.

MY EXPERIENCE WITH MORMONISM

Mormonism is a cult. I didn't know that when I married a returned Mormon missionary. All I saw was a man who was willing to give up two years of his life to travel across the ocean and share Jesus with lost souls. That was inspiring. Of course, I didn't know it was another Jesus.

Mormonism is a cult. I learned quite a lot about this false religion while I was married to a Mormon. I learned about many of the secret temple rituals and the reasons they wear special "garments" under their clothes. I learned about the angel Moroni, Joseph Smith, and the golden plates. I learned about their prophets and more.

It all seemed weird to me, but I wasn't saved at the time and I didn't know better. I remember my Baptist grandfather discussing the Mormon beliefs with my then-fiancé, trying to explain to him that Jesus—and not works—was the only way to heaven. He politely continued in his beliefs. I still didn't see that it was a false religion.

Mormonism is a cult. I went to a women's meeting at a Latter Day Saints "ward" once and attended an Easter Sunday service another time. I always had an eerie feeling when I entered that place. The people were friendly, but it felt more like a plastic persona. It felt like religion in the darkest sense of the word.

I remember when our daughter was born, my Mormon husband's Mormon parents wanted to have some strange blessing ceremony over her. I am so grateful that I said no. Even though I didn't know Mormonism was a cult—and even though I wasn't saved—something told me not to allow it.

So I thank God my Mormon husband got on a plane, supposedly to Honduras for a two-week trip, and married an El Salvadoran teenager. I thank God because I may have ended up a Mormon who believes in strange rituals, like becoming a god in eternity, and salvation by works. I thank God because I may have ended up going straight to hell.

Mormonism is a cult, and it almost sucked me in. I remember my Mormon husband telling me to read the Book of Mormon and pray about whether or not it was true. He promised me an encounter at the end of the book if I would pray—a supernatural confirmation that it was real. I started to read it, but I just couldn't stomach its contents. I never prayed that prayer, which would probably have been answered by some other spirit than the Spirit of God.

So thank God my Mormon husband abandoned me. My daughter and I both found the saving grace of the true Jesus and we may have never known the truth that set us free if we hadn't endured the pain of what at the time seemed tragic. God is good. He saw all along what was happening. When my Mormon husband abandoned us, He rescued us from the slippery slope of a false religion.

FALSE MARY WORSHIP

If you live in a region where false Mary worship is rising, you'll notice that Jezebel's witchcrafts rise again in May. That's because of the traditional "May crowning" ritual that takes place to honor the Virgin Mary as "the Queen of May."

Essentially, this means there is a hyper focus on devotions to Mary. There are two problems with this. First, Mary doesn't want or expect our devotion—she wants and expects us to worship the Son of God, Jesus. Second, by treating Mary as an idol we're empowering the spirit of Jezebel.

Although the Bible describes the mother of Jesus as "highly favored" (see Luke 1:28), that doesn't mean she is supposed to be worshiped. In fact, the Greek word for *favored* in this verse is *charitou*. *Charitou* means grace.

God honored Mary with the blessings and grace and we should respect her as the mother of Jesus but not exalt her by crowning her in rituals. We're supposed to throw our crowns at Jesus' feet (see Rev. 4:10), not place them on Mary's head.

It wasn't the disciples or apostles—not even John, whom Jesus told to care for His mother after His death on the cross (see John 19:27)—who

CLEANSING YOUR HOME FROM EVIL

started building altars to Mary. Actually, no one can trace its exact origin. Some say it started with the Greeks, who dedicated May to the goddess of fecundity known as Artemis. The Romans honored Flora, the goddess of blossoms, in May. Apparently, the notion to honor Mary along with these false gods became popular in the Middle Ages.

Many Catholics are quick to tell you they don't worship Mary or pray to Mary. But when we build an altar to Mary and adorn it with flowers and candles, are we not exalting Mary to a place that does not belong to her? Are we not worshiping the created instead of the Creator? (See Romans 1:25.)

It's curious to me that Mary, the mother of Jesus, is so often called "the queen of heaven." It's curious to me because the Bible speaks about the queen of heaven as it relates to idols. Specifically, the queen of heaven in the Bible refers to a goddess that goes by many names, including Isis, Innana, Astarte, Hera, and Asherah. As I explain in my book *The Spiritual Warrior's Guide to Defeating Jezebel*, the wicked Queen Jezebel worshiped Asherah. Jeremiah 7:17-19 warns against making altars to the queen of heaven:

> *"Do you not see what they do in the cities of Judah and in the streets of Jerusalem? The children gather wood, the fathers kindle the fire, and the women knead dough, to make cakes for the queen of heaven; and they pour out drink offerings to other gods, that they may provoke Me to anger. Do they provoke Me to anger?" says the Lord. "Do they not provoke themselves, to the shame of their own faces?"*

The Bible talks about Jezebel and her witchcrafts (2 Kings 9:22). The spirit of Jezebel is the same as Asherah (also known as Ashtoreth). The Old Testament Jezebel's father, Ethbal, was the high priest of the goddess Ashtoreth, the queen of heaven. Can you connect the dots? Mary is not the queen of May, but Jesus is the King of kings. If we're going to build an altar to anyone, it should be to our Lord and Savior, not His earthly mother.

NEWFANGLED FALSE RELIGIONS

False religions are rising just like false prophets and false christs. You've heard about converting to Judaism. But Jediisim? It's one more "ism" in a world of "isms." And it shows just how far religion has strayed from its true purpose. Hold that thought. Let's explore the world of the latest religious fad first. It's called the Temple of the Jedi Order. Its website reads:

> We are a Jedi church and international ministry of the religion Jediism and the Jedi way of life. Jedi at this site are not the same as those portrayed within the Star Wars franchise. Star Wars Jedi are fictional characters that exist within a literary and cinematic universe.

A recognized 501(c)3 non-profit organization, adherents to the Jedi faith believe in peace, justice, love, learning, and benevolence and assure the world it's unlikely its faith conflicts with other beliefs and traditions. They explain:

The Jedi here are real people that live or lived their lives according to the principles of Jediism, the real Jedi religion or philosophy. Jedi followers, ministers and leaders embrace Jediism as a real living, breathing religion and sincerely believe in its teachings. Jediism does not base its focus on myth and fiction but on the real life issues and philosophies that are at the source of myth. Whether you want to become a Jedi, are a real Jedi looking for additional training or just interested in learning about and discussing The Force, we're here for you.

Then there's Way of the Future, a new religion birthed with artificial intelligence in mind, setting up church and making news media headlines around the world. The Way of the Future is beyond humanism and evolutionist theologies. This makes a mockery of all religions and especially Christianity, using terms like Godhead. The only Way is Jesus (see John 4:6).

Beyond this is the Flying Spaghetti Monster, the deity of the Church of the Flying Spaghetti Monster. Yes, really. They call themselves Pastafarians. The point is, false gods, false religions—many which are based on humanism—are rising. Demons inspire them, and it's not a game.

DOCTRINES OF DEMONS

We know that there are deceitful spirits and teachings of demons that will lead some to depart from the faith (see 1 Tim. 4:1). We know that there are false prophets and teachers who proclaim Jesus but don't truly serve Him (see 2 Pet. 2:1). We know that satan disguises himself as an angel of light to deceive people (see 2 Cor. 11:14). And we know that some are perverting the grace of God into sensuality (see Jude 1:4).

We know all of this and yet some in the body of Christ—born-again, blood-bought, and yes, even tongue-talking—are embracing aspects of false religions. It's a subtle deception and one about which I will continue sounding the alarm until Jesus tells me not to. I'll keep sounding the alarm and speaking this truth in love in hopes that some will avoid the great falling away.

What I learned being married to a Mormon is how these deceitful spirits work. My ex-husband used to urge me to read the Book of Mormon cover to cover and then pray about whether or not it was true. Mormons promise a "burning in the bosom" will come as a confirmation when you release that prayer.

Mormons also cite James 1:5 to back up their carnal claim with actual Scripture: "If any of you lacks wisdom, let him ask of God, who gives to all liberally and without reproach, and it will be given to him." Mormons teach that any positive feelings you have after that prayer are from the Holy Spirit and any negative feelings are not from the Holy Spirit. And if you don't get the "burning in the bosom," they suggest you pray more sincerely until you do.

The New Testament is overflowing with warnings not to be deceived. Even with the Word of God, we are charged to rightly divide it (see 2 Tim. 2:15). We are in the last days. Can we really afford to let charismatic preachers, false religious gurus, and humanists tell us what the Word says? Shouldn't we be students of the Word ourselves? We all have a responsibility to guard ourselves from deception, and staying rooted in the Word of God is the best way I know to do that in this hour. It may not give you goose bumps, but it will set you free. Amen.

DEMONS HIDING BEHIND RELIGION

That's a harsh reality that should press you to get any symbols of false religion out of your house. Here is a list of false religious symbols you need to look for.

- The Book of Mormon, written by a false prophet who had an encounter with another spirit. We do not need another testament of Jesus Christ.
- Crucifixes with Jesus remaining on them—Jesus is not on the cross.
- Statues of Mary holding Jesus
- Satanic bible
- Poor Bible translations (calling God "she")
- Candles used ceremonially in rituals
- Statues of saints
- "The wheel of the law," which looks like a wheel, is a symbol used in Hinduism, Jainism, and Buddhism.
- Statute of the angel Moroni, used by the Mormons
- Mormon Star and Crescent
- Triskelion, a Celtic symbol used with neopaganistic religions

- Om, considered a sacred syllable used in Hindu prayers and mantras

- Eye of Horas, which is also known as a wadjet. It is an ancient Egyptian symbol that looks like an eye with decorations surrounding it.

- Swastika—an ancient religious icon also used by Adolph Hitler's Nazi Germany

- Pentagram—a five-pointed star originally used in ancient Greece and Babylon but now used by satanists and witches

There are too many religious symbols to list here. You'll find them often in jewelry, in pottery, and they may not look religious at all. For example, the Happy Human symbol just looks like a man raising his hands, but it's a secular icon for humanists. The winged heart, also called a Tughra Inayati, looks innocent enough, but it's an old Sufi symbol. Sufi is Islamic mysticism. My rule is, if anything has a weird symbol on it, it goes.

CHAPTER 11

BLACK MAGIC

AND OCCULT MATERIALS

A t first, I thought it was New Age culture. But I was wrong. It was occultism.

As I strolled through the streets of Key West on a 24-hour getaway with my daughter, I noticed something that I had never witnessed in Key West before—occultism seems fully woven through the culture.

I've been going to Key West for more than 20 years and have spent weeks at a time on the tropical island. But something disturbing has happened in the 10 years since I last visited—and it's merely a microcosm of what's happening in the world today.

You can no longer walk down Duval Street—the famous drag of shops and restaurants—without running into the likes of Mahadeo Jerrybandhan, a renowned "peerless palmist" from Trinidad with a long white beard and an even longer white robe. But Jerrybandhan is not alone. He has plenty of peers in Key West, from psychics to mediums to channels to healers to tarot card readers to astrologers. The only group I didn't find down there were the crystal readers.

Then there's "Robert the Doll." Key West profiteers have designed so-called ghost tours that explore the haunted history of Key West, including old wooden houses where spirits purportedly walk. Tour guides will tell you that Key West is one of the most haunted cities in the world with elevated paranormal activity. A local voodooistic icon, Robert the Doll will supposedly curse you if you take his picture without permission or forget to thank him for the privilege.

THE ABOMINATION OF OCCULTISM

As you can imagine, seeing all this grieved my spirit. But I should not have been so surprised. Occultism has been slowly creeping into American culture for decades as movie makers exalt witchcraft and vampires while the music industry pumps occult rock. Beloved, we are in the midst of a great spiritual crisis even now. Our literature, music, video games, comics, films, and television shows are full of mysticism and the occult. Some of it is subtle. Some of it is blatant. All of it is wicked.

Again, this is nothing new. Occultism—which broadly includes magic, séances, channeling, hypnosis, necromancy, astrology, extra-sensory perception, alchemy, spiritualism, and divination—is strongly condemned in the Bible.

> *There shall not be found among you anyone who makes his son or his daughter pass through the fire* [which is an ancient occult

practice], *or one who practices witchcraft, or a soothsayer, or one who interprets omens, or a sorcerer, or one who conjures spells, or a medium, or a spiritist, or one who calls up the dead. For all who do these things are an abomination to the Lord* (Deuteronomy 18:10-12).

The Lord rebuked Israel for practicing astrology (see Isa. 47:10-14). Jezebel practiced witchcraft (see 2 Kings 9:22), and we know how that ended. Ephesus was known for a population that practiced magic arts (see Acts 19:19). And the book of Revelation makes it clear that "the cowardly, unbelieving, abominable, murderers, sexually immoral, sorcerers, idolaters, and all liars shall have their part in the lake which burns with fire and brimstone, which is the second death" (Rev. 21:8).

But we should not be surprised. The rise of occultism is a sign of the end times. Satan's plan is to fascinate our hearts with occult power and deceive us. The Holy Spirit, meanwhile, wants to fascinate our spirits with a revelation of the Son of God. I believe God's people are enticed by occultism when they begin seeking spiritual experiences above seeking God. It's a subtle—and dangerous—shift. Many Christians are on fire for God, but that fire can suddenly turn strange if we are not rooted in the Word. If we seek supernatural experiences, we will find them—but they don't always come from Jesus.

Beloved, we must not play with strange fire. Ultimately, the occult leads to murder and mayhem—immorality of all kinds. It's not likely that you would ever willfully visit the likes of Mahadeo Jerrybandhan, the peerless palmist—or any of his peers. But could you ignorantly be engaged with occultic practices that are opening the door to deceptive dangers? Could it be coming from what appears to be godly influences—even within church culture?

DISCERNMENT OR DECEPTION?

Don't brush the question off before praying about it. If you want the truth, the Holy Spirit will lead you and guide you into all truth. Please hear me! Even a little occult is a deadly poison—a little leaven leavens the whole lump. The Bible warns about deceptive teachers, false apostles, and deceitful workers. The Bible warns about self-deception. And it's your responsibility to keep your heart pure. If you've stepped into this demonic ditch, repent now and warn others.

Friends, we're in an end-times war with eternal consequences. Satan is using the occult to seduce people away from the kingdom of God to dance in the kingdom of darkness. I pray that the Lord gives you discernment and awakens your spirit, for you do not know on what day your Lord is coming (see Matt. 24:42). Let me leave you with a warning from the apostle Paul:

> Beware lest anyone cheat you through philosophy and empty deceit, according to the tradition of men, according to the basic principles of the world, and not according to Christ (Colossians 2:8).

Black magic and occult materials are creating spiritual climates that are laden with witchcraft. Witchcraft is the power of the devil and causes many symptoms, from confusion and forgetfulness to irritability and infirmity.

What you don't resist can influence you, so when you invite symbols of black magic and the occult into your home, troublesome things happen. That's because you are in some level of agreement with dark powers, and what you agree with can influence you.

At best, you may see strife manifest in your home or signs of what might seem like a haunted house, with items moving from place to place and strange sounds or eerie feelings. At worst, you could wind up with mental health issues, marriage issues, money issues, and all sorts of other serious issues.

WOE TO THE WITCHCRAFT

Put another way, when you practice witchcraft you bring woe into your life.

> *Thus says the Lord God: "Woe to the women who sew magic charms on their sleeves and make veils for the heads of people of every height to hunt souls! Will you hunt the souls of My people, and keep yourselves alive?"* (Ezekiel 13:18)

What was going on here? According to the Geneva Study Bible, "These superstitious women for lucre [money] would prophesy and tell every man his fortune, giving them pillows to lean upon, and kerchiefs to cover their heads, to the intent they might the more allure them and bewitch them." And what is woe? Woe is ruinous trouble, calamity, and affliction, according to *Merriam-Webster*'s dictionary.

You don't have to be practicing witchcraft to come into agreement with it. Think about it this way. You wouldn't knowingly invite a psychic into your home to show off her palm-reading skills. But by bringing black magic and occult materials into your home, you are in that same level of agreement. And, again, we can't claim ignorance. The devil is legalistic, and Paul warns us not to be ignorant of the devil's devices (see 2 Cor. 2:11).

IT'S CALLED BLACK MAGIC FOR A REASON

Black magic is called black magic for a reason. *Merriam-Webster*'s defines it as magic that is associated with the devil or with evil spirits and also calls it evil magic. This is not the type of magic that's a sleight of hand à la Houdini or, in modern terms, David Copperfield or Penn & Teller. These are not illusions but demons.

By contrast, white magic is also witchcraft. Dictionary.com defines white magic as "magic used for good purposes, especially to counteract evil." Remember the show *Bewitched*? Samantha was a good witch and her mother, Endora, was an evil witch. They would combat each other with witchcraft powers. But witchcraft is witchcraft. A cat is a cat no matter what color or how many stripes it has—or how you skin it. That means even games, dolls, or pictures of witches must not be in your home.

THE SECRECY OF THE OCCULT

The occult uses witchcraft, but the occult is more than witchcraft. *Occult*, by definition, means to shut off from view or exposure, not revealed, secret, not easily apprehended or understood, abstruse, mysterious, or concealed, according to *Merriam-Webster*'s dictionary. Another definition is "matters regarded as involving the action or influence of supernatural or supernormal powers or some secret knowledge of them."

Many practices fall under the occult. Indeed, too many to list here. But here's a few—astrology, calling up the dead, Celtic religion, Freemasonry, mirror gazing, omens, Ouija boards, secret societies, voodoo, spirit guides, and tea cup reading.

FREEMASONRY'S BONDAGE

It's worth a little more explanation on Freemasonry. The word "free" in its nomenclature is itself deceptive. Freemasonry puts people into bondage. You may not be familiar with freemasonry, so let's define it.

Freemasonry disguises itself as "the leading fraternal organization in the world. Its origins are lost in the unrecorded history of medieval times, but it formally organized in London, England, in 1717. ...As a fraternal organization, Freemasonry unites men of good character who, though of different religious, ethnic or social backgrounds, share a belief in the fatherhood of God and the brotherhood of mankind."[1]

First, this is not a Christian organization, but many Christians are active practitioners of what is essentially a mystic religion. This is a secret society and has seen spin-off groups like the Shriners and Eastern Star. Lutheran Church Missouri Synod wrote, "It is because tenets and practices of Freemasonry conflict with the biblical Gospel of Jesus Christ that our church from its very beginning has held that membership in this organization conflicts with a faithful confession of this Gospel."[2]

The Southern Baptist Convention wrote, "The heresy of universalism (the belief all people will eventually be saved) which permeates the writings of many Masonic authors, which is a doctrine inconsistent with New Testament teaching."[3] And the Assemblies of God wrote, "Confidence in these secret orders and their teachings has always tended toward the embracing of a false hope of salvation through good works and improved moral service (Ephesians 2:8-9)."[4]

We could stack up objection after objection from the church about Freemasonry, including the omission of Jesus Christ from biblical texts they use in their secret rituals, promoting false claims about God, taking secret oaths that are incompatible with Scripture's encouragement of the fellowship of the saints, and more. Yet many Christians practice Freemasonry and have masonic symbols in their homes.

Freemason practices defy Scripture. Paul wrote: "Beware lest anyone cheat you through philosophy and empty deceit, according to the tradition of men, according to the basic principles of the world, and not according to Christ" (Col. 2:8).

So what qualifies as black magic symbols that may be in your home, on your clothes, or elsewhere? Given its secrecy, you may be surprised at some of the occult symbols.

- Voodoo dolls
- The Rose Cross, a cross with a rose on it
- Pyramid (used by Freemasons and Illuminati)
- Tree of Life (associated with Kabala)
- All-Seeing Eye

THE SIGILLUM DEI, SEAL OF THE TRUTH OF GOD

- Robert Fludd sketches, such as the Created Universe as Reflection of God and the Macrocosm and Microcosm
- The evil eye (often sold as jewelry or decorations)
- Hieroglyphic Monad, a stick figure drawing of an entity that birthed all things
- Lightning bolt (seen as 777 by satanists)
- Snake skin
- Ritual candles
- Graveyard dirt
- Cauldrons
- Protection amulets
- Zodiac man, depicting zodiacal names with body parts
- Baphomet, a deity that looks like a man with a goat face and wings, horns, and a beard
- Black Sun (Nazism and Neo-Nazi movement)

- Circled dot

- Icelandic magical staves

In essence, anything used to cast a spell or anything that has occult symbols on it needs to be removed from your home. Moon or constellation jewelry falls into this category. The list really goes on and on. If something carries a strange symbol you don't understand, it should not be in your home.

NOTES

1. "What Is Freemasonry?" The Grand Lodge of Ohio, accessed March 20, 2021, https://www.freemason.com/join/what-is -freemasonry.

2. The Lutheran Church Missouri Synod, "Frequently Asked Questions—LCMS Views," accessed March 20, 2021, https:// www.lcms.org/about/beliefs/faqs/lcms-views#masons.

3. "Freemasonry Overview," North American Mission Board, Seventh Incompatibility, March 30, 2016, https://www.namb .net/apologetics/resource/freemasonry-overview.

4. "Minutes of the 58th Session of the General Council of the Assemblies of God," Orlando, FL, August 1-4, 2019, https:// ag.org/About/About-the-AG/Constitution-and-Bylaws.

CHAPTER 12

WHAT'S IN
YOUR KID'S ROOM?

've told you the story about my daughter in the bathtub. After that, I was extremely vigilant about what came in the house. I went through her entire room looking for more snakes, turtles, and toys that could open her up to demonic attack.

Children are especially vulnerable to demonic attack if their parents are ignorant of the devil's devices. The enemy enjoys taking advantage of children, leaving his marks on their precious souls while they are especially impressionable. We see this through the media, but also the toys with which they play.

Proverbs 22:6 admonishes us, "Train up a child in the way he should go, and when he is old he will not depart from it." If we train them up to play with toys that have demonic connotations or open them up to perverted influences, we could find that they fall away from the Lord for a season when they are older. By contrast, when your children are taught by the Lord, their peace is great (see Isa. 54:13).

Your children may resist you getting rid of toys that carry curses and evil, but you have to remember that God gave their souls to you to steward. Proverbs 29:15 says the child left to himself brings shame to his mother. Proverbs 22:15 tells us folly is bound up in the heart of a child. And Proverbs 29:17 assures us if we discipline our children they will bring delight to our heart.

Taking away toys that carry curses is not a discipline against them; it's training them in righteousness. Be prepared to let them go shopping for new toys so they are not provoked to anger and discouragement. Explain to them as best you can (and without scaring them) why you have to take the toys out of the home. You'll have to give them an age-appropriate explanation. If they are under four years old, you can probably just replace the toys with godly toys without much inquisition.

FANTASIES AND MYTHOLOGIES

Paul warned in Second Timothy 4:3-4, "For the time will come when they will not endure sound doctrine, but according to their own desires, because they have itching ears, they will heap up for themselves teachers; and they will turn their ears away from the truth, and be turned aside to fables." The New International Version says, "turn aside to myths." The New Living Translation says, "chase after myths."

Merriam-Webster's dictionary defines *fantasy* as "imaginative fiction featuring especially strange settings and grotesque characters." And a *myth* is defined as "usually a traditional story of ostensibly historical events that serves to unfold part of the world view of a people or explain a practice, belief or natural phenomenon."

Remember, Paul was battling the Greek and Roman mythology of his day with the gospel of Christ. Toys that depict fantastic creatures and mythological gods have no place in a Christian home. If you investigated the origin of some of these toys, including puppets, you would find they are rooted in false deities.

Some of these toys include trolls, Rainbow Brite and Sprite, Smurfs (the German word for *wizard* is *smurf*). Cabbage Patch Kids, elves, fairies, Pegasus, gremlins, mermaids, dragons, and the like. Many fantasy or mythological creatures look like demons. Children who are allowed to idolize fantasies and mythological creatures can open themselves up to demonic attack. Romans 1:22-23 tells us, "Claiming to be wise, they instead became utter fools. And instead of worshiping the glorious, ever-living God, they worshiped idols made to look like mere people and birds and animals and reptiles" (NLT).

DEMONIC GAMES

Many of us grew up with toys like Monopoly or Chutes and Ladders. Today, there are demonic board games and video games. Beyond Ouija boards—which are boards printed with letters, numbers, and signs with a game piece that moves over the board to spell out answers to questions in a séance setting—there's Dungeons and Dragons.

Dungeons and Dragons is a fantasy role-playing game in which players are characters in a fantasy story that never ends. One story is "Icewind Dale: Rime of the Frostmaiden." The game includes occultic elements. According to Focus on the Family, "Some former players have said that 'D & D' brought them into contact with demonic activity. Such claims need to be taken very seriously."[1]

Other board games to watch for are *The Witching Hour, Exceed Seventh Cross: Hunters vs. Demons, Doom*, and *Dark Souls*. Of course, violent video games should also be on your hunt list. Fantasy board games should be a no go in your household.

LGBT TOYS

The LGBT community has penetrated the entertainment industry, and that includes clothing, toys, and books. Although the rainbow belongs to a God as a sign of His covenant with man, the LGBT community has taken it as a sign of pride. The covers of books like *Prince & Knight, Julian is a Mermaid,* and *A Day in the Life of Marlon Bundo* may seem innocent, but the contents are perverse.

The Bible makes it clear, "You shall not lie with a male as with a woman. It is an abomination" (Lev. 18:22). In the New Testament we read, "Likewise also the men, leaving the natural use of the woman, burned in their lust for one another, men with men committing what is shameful, and receiving in themselves the penalty of their error which was due" (Rom. 1:27).

There are also LGBT dolls, Legos, and action figures. Some of them include the Sally Ride minifigure, the Lance Bass marionette, the Elton

John singing doll, and the Boy George doll. Some are less obvious, like the Robbie Rogers minifigure, a gay soccer player, and Michael Sam, the first outed gay player drafted into the NFL.

Be careful about the action figures you buy your children. They could have homosexual connotations. For example, in the movie *Toy Story 4*, Spork is transgender.

TOYS AND BOOKS PROMOTING MAGIC AND WITCHCRAFT

Anything promoting magic powers can carry an evil spirit. Magic kits, magic 8 balls that tell the future, toys that open children up to the supernatural, wizards, even E.T., who is an extraterrestrial being who levitates, and Yoda, a Zen master in Star Wars, are suspect.

Authors are even targeting children with witchcraft books. Beyond Harry Potter, there are books like *The Junior Witch's Handbook: A Kid's Guide to White Magic, Spells and Rituals* and *The Magikal Family*, and *Where to Park Your Broomstick: A Teens' Guide to Witchcraft*. You may never bring these things into your home, but your children can have them in their backpacks without you knowing it.

NOTE

1. Focus on the Family, "Teen Questions About "Dungeons and Dragons," 2010, https://www.focusonthefamily.com/family-qa/teen-questions-about-dungeons-and-dragons.

CHAPTER 13

DEMONS

CAN HIDE ANYWHERE

Did you know seemingly innocent objects can carry wicked agendas? The enemy is sneaky. In fact, God said of the serpent that he was "more subtle" than any other animal (see Gen. 3:1). Indeed, a painting, a purse, or a decorative object in your house could seem harmless and even beautiful but can carry demons. Indeed, in many cases evil is hiding in plain sight.

Evil symbols can be on mugs, posters, or bumper stickers on your car. Evil symbols or objects can come into your home through well-meaning gifts or even the mailman's delivery. You can find evil lurking on CD covers, magazine advertisements, logos on products you consume regularly, T-shirts, and jewelry.

Sometimes it's nothing you brought in. There could even been demons left behind in the darkness from what the former residents did in the home, evil sins or objects left behind. It's important to leave no stone unturned. If an object, emblem, or logo doesn't feel right, get rid of it. If you don't know what a symbol means, look it up.

SECRET SOCIETY EMBLEMS

We talked briefly about Freemasons, which is one of many secret societies. There are a slew of masonic symbols you may overlook in everyday life. The Masonic square and compasses emblem with a "G" in the middle is actually copyrighted. But that's not the only emblem associated with Freemasonry.

Secret societies are antichrist. Colossians 2:8, in an indirect way that actually is very clear, says, "Beware lest anyone cheat you through philosophy and empty deceit, according to the tradition of men, according to the basic principles of the world, and not according to Christ." What's deceiving is some of the Freemasonry symbols, like the Lodge of Protection, use Hebrew letters.

The Eastern Star represents an order within the Freemasons. It's a five-pointed star with blue, red, green, and white points. Other orders of the Freemasons have their own emblems, such as the Rainbow Girls, the Scottish Rite, and the DeMolay Emblem. There's even a symbol they call the Eye of God, which is really the equivalent to the All Seeing Eye (and it's rooted in the occult).

Other secret societies include the Illuminati, which uses a symbol of a pyramid with an eye in the middle. There's the Skull and Bones Society, represented by a skull and bones. The list goes on with the Ordo Templi Oreintis, the Priory of Sion, the Ancient Mystical Order of Rosae Crucis,

Carbonari, the Hermetic Brotherhood of Life, and so on. Most of these symbols do not look altogether evil at first glance.

We'll leave it there because Ephesians 5:11-12 tells us, "And have no fellowship with the unfruitful works of darkness, but rather expose them. For it is shameful even to speak of those things which are done by them in secret."

HALLOWEEN COSTUMES

Not just for children, Halloween costumes can seem like all good fun but can open your home to demons. Fairies, witches, ghouls, devils, the Grim Reaper, vampires, and other depictions of evil should not be found in your home. When you dress this way—or allow your children to dress this way—you are fellowshipping and even promoting works of darkness.

Paul warned in Second Corinthians 6:14 that light has no fellowship with darkness. Romans 13:12 calls us to lay aside the deeds of darkness and put on the armor of light. There's nothing wrong, in essence, with costume parties. When I was a little girl, my mother dressed me up as an angel. It wasn't a store-bought costume either. She made it by hand, with tin foil wings and everything! What is dangerous is imitating evil. John warned us not to imitate evil but imitate good (see 3 John 1:11).

Ultimately, we are not supposed to conform to the ways of the world but to the ways of God and walk as children of light (see Eph. 5:6-12). There is no darkness in God, so we should not celebrate darkness (see 1 John 1:5). Satan, as I have said throughout this book, masquerades himself—or puts on a costume that makes him appear as an angel of light. Dark Halloween costumes may seem like all fun and games, but in reality it's opening us up to demonic attacks. First Thessalonians 5:22 tells us to reject every kind of evil.

CONSUMER PRODUCT LOGOS

Many products we bring into our home have logos rooted in mythology. Pegasus, for example, is a symbol for Mercury the messenger god. FTD® Flowers uses this symbol. The American Medical Association uses the caduceus symbol. Caduceus is the staff the Greek god Hermes carried. Nike shoes carry the symbol of Athena, the goddess of victory.

You don't want to be paranoid, but you do want to be educated. I'll say it over and over again. If there's a strange symbol on a product, investigate it before bringing it into your home. It's not a matter of being legalistic; it's a matter of not being ignorant of the devil's devices (see 2 Cor. 2:11).

CHAPTER 14

HOW TO FIND
EVIL IN YOUR HOME

You may be aware of one or two objects in your home that are blatantly staring you in the face at this point, just daring you to evict them. But the question is, what else is lurking in the closets, attics, cupboards, and storage places that you have long forgotten about?

When we move from one home to another, we usually throw some things away—like old clothes, broken appliances, or stuff we haven't used in ten years—but we tend to have mementos stored in chests or boxes that we rarely, if ever, dive back into. We all have boxes of precious memories, but even those precious memories could be mingled with cursed objects.

Cleansing your home from evil can be a tedious process. How thorough you are depends on how serious you are about dismantling the devil's agenda for your life. Again, the obvious frog on the shelf is an easy target. But if you want to be totally free you may have to get your hands dirty, so to speak, digging through every nook and cranny of your home until you feel a clearance in the spirit.

Think of it this way. When I hire maid services, most of them do a surface-level job. They don't take all the knickknacks off the shelf to dust—they just wipe around them. They don't take the books off the shelf. They just sweep across the edge of the shelf, leaving a slight line of dust at the edge of the books. My mother always made me take everything off the shelves to clean and go inside the corners of the cabinets when wiping things down.

If you do a surface-level spiritual cleansing of your home, you could miss something critical at worst or, at best, leave residue that still causes problems. Likely, you will have to do this in stages to do a deep sweep through your home. Start with that low-hanging fruit, but don't neglect the potentially more nefarious demons hiding in the dark places.

With all that said, you may decide some of what was mentioned in this book was too extreme. You don't want to lose the owls or let go of the Nike shoes. This is not intended to be a religious exercise or to feel extreme. But know that the enemy is an extremist. He is a terrorist. He is a legalist. If you are desperate for freedom, please don't ignore what you feel is harmless when Scripture indicates the danger or when the Holy Spirit gives you check in your spirit. It doesn't have to make sense to your mind. The following is my process for finding evil in your home.

PRAY FOR GOD TO REVEAL ANYTHING IN YOUR HOME

Start with prayer. Pray and ask God to reveal any evil in in your home. God is all-knowing. He knows where every accursed object is and He is as passionate about evicting demons from your home as you are. You may have forgotten about that innocent-looking evil object, but He didn't. Pray this prayer:

> Father, in the name of Jesus, as I set out to cleanse my home from evil help me not to leave any demons behind. Remind me of items I purchased or gifts I received that may be attracting devils or curses into my house. Show me items I might overlook because I don't see the harm in them. Help me hear Your voice and recognize Your nudge as I endeavor to evict demon powers that are plaguing my household.

Now, before you start searching, stop for a few minutes and wait on the Lord. Perk your spiritual ears up. Have a pen and paper in hand in case He tells or shows you something. He may not speak directly to you in this way, but then again He may. Give Him the opportunity before you go on your demon hunt.

The Holy Spirit may show you what room to start with or what items to start with. If by some chance you don't hear anything, just start with the obvious items. If He doesn't instruct you otherwise, your bedroom is a good place to start because it's an intimate place in your home and it's a place of vulnerability because you are asleep.

Next, walk around your house quietly and slowly and look around with your natural eyes. God may illuminate something to you, or He may give you a direct instruction as you prayer walk through your house with eyes and ears wide open. Follow His instructions.

GET THE REST OF YOUR FAMILY INVOLVED

If you live in a large home or if you have a house full of people, you'll want to get the rest of the family involved—at least those who understand the concept of cleansing your home. Explain this process to them. Fill them in on what you learned. Let them read this book. You don't want family members resisting your efforts to get rid of accursed objects, so don't skip this step. You need all eyes and all hands on deck.

To be sure, cleansing your home needs to be a unified effort, if at all possible. If there is a member of your family who is not in agreement, leave them out of the search and maintain peace. In First Corinthians 1:10 Paul writes, "Now I plead with you, brethren, by the name of our Lord Jesus Christ, that you all speak the same thing, and that there be no divisions among you, but that you be perfectly joined together in the same mind and in the same judgment."

If you have a teenager or unsaved family member who has brought items into your home that are contrary to your faith, remember that you have authority in your home. I am not suggesting you go to war with a spouse over an item they hold dear. With spouses, it's a more difficult situation and a matter of prayer that they will see things the way the Lord does. In any case, if you can get most of the accursed objects out of your house you may have an easier time with the unbelieving spouse going forward because the level of evil in the home is lesser. But with children—even grown children who are still at home—you can put your foot down.

Start with the low-hanging fruit.

I mentioned this before, but I don't mind repeating it. Start with the low-hanging fruit, unless the Holy Spirit instructs otherwise. Starting with the low-hanging fruit can make you feel like you accomplished something and encourage you to keep going. It can also provide some measure of relief from the demonic activity in your home.

Now that your eyes have been opened, you will start to see the obvious things in your home. You may see salt and pepper shakers depicting owls. You may see a movie in your library that has no business in a Christian's home. You may see engravings on what are otherwise cute jewelry boxes. You may see clothes in your closet with demonic symbols.

Dig through the closets.

When I say dig, I mean dig. While writing this I cleaned through two of my closets and threw out bags and bags of stuff. None of it carried accursed objects, but I really wasn't sure what I might find. Even if you don't find anything in your storage closets, bedroom closets, utility closets, and the like, you'll feel good about how nice and neat everything is when you're done. You'll have more room and less clutter.

Look in your media cabinet.

The media cabinet—if you have one, or you may keep these things in closets—is a hotbed for magazines, CDs, DVDs, board games, and similar items that may carry demonic objects. Not all secular music or movies have demonic undertones, but many do. As I mentioned earlier, when I was born again, I instinctively threw away all my worldly movies and CDs. I knew nothing about cleansing my home from evil. It just became repulsive to me, so I discarded it all.

Look in the basement and attics or sheds if you have them.

Attics, sheds, and basements are for deep storage. You store things there you don't expect to have to put your hands on for a long, long time. This makes the perfect breeding ground for demonic parties. The psalmist wrote, "For the dark places of the earth are full of the haunts of cruelty" (Ps. 74:20).

Who knows? You might find things in there that don't even belong to you. People who lived in the home before you may have left accursed objects behind unknowingly. Basements, attics, and sheds are perhaps some of the most likely sources of ongoing demonic trouble because the contents are out of sight and out of mind.

Scan through old photo albums.

Yes, old pictures of your past sinful life are leaving an open door. Look through your photo albums. If there are photos of you engaging in sinful behaviors, gather them up for the fire. If there are photos of old boyfriends or girlfriends with whom you have soul ties, gather them up for the fire. If it's not glorifying God, if it's depicting a work of the flesh, gather them up for the fire. You are a new creation. That's not you anymore. Galatians 5:19-21 reads:

Now the works of the flesh are evident, which are: adultery, fornication, uncleanness, lewdness, idolatry, sorcery, hatred, contentions, jealousies, outbursts of wrath, selfish ambitions, dissensions, heresies, envy, murders, drunkenness, revelries, and the like; of which I tell you beforehand, just as I also told you in time past, that those who practice such things will not inherit the kingdom of God.

As a side note, if you've made a shrine out of photos and objects from dead loved ones, it is time to disassemble the shrine. You can attract familiar spirits if your purpose for having photos and reminders is not rooted in the right kind of love. Grief can attract familiar spirits. So while it may seem innocent, it could be dangerous. There's nothing wrong with having a photo of your dead parents on the table. But when it's a shrine—when it's a place of devotion or lingering memories that bring sorrow—it's not healthy.

Look in your backyard, in your gardens, etc.

Go into your backyard. Look in your gardens. Are there mermaid fountains, frog ornaments, and other evil statues in your yard? These evil objects may not be inside your home yet, but they are nevertheless on your property and are attracting evil. There are plenty of pleasant decorations you can use in your garden. Take this as an opportunity to pick out some new items.

Go to your storage facility.

If you have a storage facility, put that on your list of stops. Although it's not technically in your house, any items found there are legally in your ownership. Just because it's not in your house doesn't mean you want it in your possession.

Look through your car.

Most people spend a good deal of time in their car. You may have an air freshener hanging from the rearview mirror you need to dispose of because of what it depicts. You may have junk in the trunk you forgot about.

Scan your office at work.

What about your desk at work? Your drawers? You don't want accursed objects anywhere near you. You can't control the entire work environment, but you can be responsible for your corner.

LOOK, CLEANSE, REPEAT

I've discovered some people actually have to go through this process more than once because they missed something they didn't think was harmful. It's better to go slow, asking the Holy Spirit along the way to identify objects that grieve Him or that carry curses, than it is to have to start from top to bottom a second time.

As you are looking for objects, play worship music in your home, pray in the spirit, sing songs to the Lord, praise and thank His name. Start even now cultivating that atmosphere of God's stronghold as you prepare to evict the enemy.

CHAPTER 15

WHAT TO DO WITH

WHAT YOU FIND

So, you've pored through your house, your car, your shed, your attic, your basement, your backyard, and you have gathered bags of accursed objects. What do you do now? Whatever you do, don't give them to Goodwill. Don't be the one who causes curses to come into another household. You need to burn them with fire, if at all possible. This is biblical. In fact, several scriptures point to burning the objects with fire. Deuteronomy 7:25-26 tells us plainly:

> *You shall burn the carved images of their gods with fire; you shall not covet the silver or gold that is on them, nor take it for yourselves, lest you be snared by it; for it is an abomination to the Lord your God. Nor shall you bring an abomination into*

*your house, lest you be doomed to destruction like it. You shall
utterly detest it and utterly abhor it, for it is an accursed thing.*

And again:

*But thus you shall deal with them: you shall destroy their
altars, and break down their sacred pillars, and cut down
their wooden images, and burn their carved images with fire*
(Deuteronomy 7:5).

And again:

*And you shall destroy their altars, break their sacred pillars,
and burn their wooden images with fire; you shall cut down
the carved images of their gods and destroy their names from
that place* (Deuteronomy 12:3).

When the Israelites made a golden calf to worship while Moses was
on Mount Sinai receiving the Ten Commandments from Jehovah, the
prophet did not stop with burning the accursed object with fire. Exodus
32:20 says, "Then he took the calf which they had made, burned it in the
fire, and ground it to powder; and he scattered it on the water and made
the children of Israel drink it."

BURNED WITH FIRE

Burning cursed objects with fire is not just an Old Testament thing.
We see the same practice in the New Testament. In the Book of Acts, we

read about the apostle Paul's exploits in Ephesus. Acts 19:11-20 gives the account of power encounters, miracles, revival, and burning accursed objects.

> *Now God worked unusual miracles by the hands of Paul, so that even handkerchiefs or aprons were brought from his body to the sick, and the diseases left them and the evil spirits went out of them. Then some of the itinerant Jewish exorcists took it upon themselves to call the name of the Lord Jesus over those who had evil spirits, saying, "We exorcise you by the Jesus whom Paul preaches." Also there were seven sons of Sceva, a Jewish chief priest, who did so.*
>
> *And the evil spirit answered and said, "Jesus I know, and Paul I know; but who are you?"*
>
> *Then the man in whom the evil spirit was leaped on them, overpowered them, and prevailed against them, so that they fled out of that house naked and wounded. This became known both to all Jews and Greeks dwelling in Ephesus; and fear fell on them all, and the name of the Lord Jesus was magnified. And many who had believed came confessing and telling their deeds. Also, many of those who had practiced magic brought their books together and burned them in the sight of all. And they counted up the value of them, and it totaled fifty thousand pieces of silver. So the word of the Lord grew mightily and prevailed.*

Why burn accursed objects? When you burn something, it's utterly destroyed. There is no more sign of it. It has no more power. When you burn the accursed object with fire, it's a symbol of the devil's everlasting torment in the lake of fire. Again, don't give it away and pass the curses on to someone else. Don't sell it and profit off evil. Burn it.

Some objects can't be burned, but they can still be destroyed. Smash glass objects. Deface idols that can't be burned. Make the item unusable, irreparable, and unattractive and dispose of it. Do the item enough damage that if anyone finds it, they will not want it. This may seem aggressive to you, but if you want aggressive demons to loose your home and leave your life, you need to get violent in the spirit. After all, Jesus said, "The kingdom of heaven suffers violence, and the violent take it by force" (Matt. 11:12).

REPENTING AND RENOUNCING

Once you have dealt with the accursed object itself, it's time to evict the enemy. First, you need repent to God for bringing these items or allowing these items into your home and renounce all involvement with the evil. You are the gatekeeper of your home. Ignorance is no excuse as Paul warned us not to be ignorant of the devil's devices (see 2 Cor. 2:11).

Know this: God is not mad at you. Quite the contrary; He is pleased that you are cleansing your home from evil. He is overjoyed that you are rejecting the enemy. Repentance is a gift freely, generously, and kindly offered. We need to learn to walk in a lifestyle of repentance. If you are practicing sin, you won't successfully maintain victory over the enemy.

Proverbs 28:13 says, "He who covers his sins will not prosper, but whoever confesses and forsakes them will have mercy." And First John

1:8-10 tells us: "If we say that we have no sin, we deceive ourselves, and the truth is not in us. If we confess our sins, He is faithful and just to forgive us our sins and to cleanse us from all unrighteousness. If we say that we have not sinned, we make Him a liar, and His word is not in us." Psalm 24:3-5 says:

Who may ascend the mountain of the Lord? Who may stand in his holy place? The one who has clean hands and a pure heart, who does not trust in an idol or swear by a false god. They will receive blessing from the Lord and vindication from God their Savior (NIV).

And in a telling letter to the church at Corinth that followed a stern letter of rebuke, Paul wrote:

For even if I made you sorry with my letter, I do not regret it; though I did regret it. For I perceive that the same epistle made you sorry, though only for a while. Now I rejoice, not that you were made sorry, but that your sorrow led to repentance. For you were made sorry in a godly manner, that you might suffer loss from us in nothing. For godly sorrow produces repentance leading to salvation, not to be regretted; but the sorrow of the world produces death. For observe this very thing, that you sorrowed in a godly manner: What diligence it produced in you, what clearing of yourselves, what indignation, what fear, what vehement desire, what zeal, what vindication! In all things you proved yourselves to be clear in this matter. Therefore, although I wrote to you, I did not do it for the sake of him who had done the wrong, nor for the sake of him who suffered wrong, but that our care for you in the sight of God might appear to you (2 Corinthians 7:8-12).

We all fall short of the glory of God every day. Repentance itself can cause the warfare to stop because we are resisting the devil and submitting ourselves to God. When we do this, according to James 4:7, he has to flee. Pray this prayer:

Father, in the name of Jesus, forgive me for bring accursed objects into Your home. Forgive me for celebrating darkness. Forgive me for my ignorance concerning the devil's devices. Cleanse me from all affiliation and residue from contact with unrighteousness. Give me greater discernment so I can avoid the snares of the enemy, in Jesus' name.

CHAPTER 16

YOU HAVE
AUTHORITY

The devil does not have the authority God gave you in Christ. God has authorized you—He's given you authority. Again, Jesus boldly proclaimed, "All authority has been given to Me in heaven and on earth" (Matt. 28:18). Jesus is not a man that He should lie. He wasn't boasting or speaking things that are not as though they were. Jesus is the Co-Creator of the universe. He has preeminence. He has all authority.

One meaning of *exousia*, the Greek word for *authority* in that verse, reads: "the power of rule or government (the power of him whose will and commands must be submitted to by others and obeyed." That sums up Christ's authority.

God raised Christ from the dead by the power of the Holy Spirit and seated Him at His right hand in heavenly places:

> *Far above all principality and power and might and domin-*
> *ion, and every name that is named, not only in this age but also*

in that which is to come. And He put all things under His feet, and gave Him to be head over all things to the church, which is His body, the fullness of Him who fills all in all (Ephesians 1:21-23).

Now, we are seated with Christ in heavenly places (see Eph. 2:6). If you are born again, you have been delivered from the power of darkness and translated into Christ's Kingdom (see Col. 1:13). You've been translated from the enemy's authority and rule of government into Christ's authority and rule of government.

If you don't understand who you are in Christ—if you don't understand your authority in Him—you cannot successfully wage war against the enemy who is waging war against you in or outside of your home.

YOU ARE AUTHORIZED

Just like Adam had authority before he handed it over to the devil through his disobedience in the Garden of Eden, we now have authority in Christ to take dominion in the spirit realm over enemies of the cross. Jesus gave His disciples a measure of His own authority, jurisdiction, influence, and anointing to so they could go about doing good and heal all who were oppressed by the devil (see Acts 10:38).

Like the disciples, God has authorized you to stand against the enemy. *Merriam-Webster* offers the world's definition of authority: "power of influence to command a thought, opinion, or behavior." But the Greek word for *authority* in the Bible is *exousia*, which includes the concept of "authorization."

Authority is the power to act on God's Word. When God speaks, we're authorized to move. When you are authorized you are commissioned, certified, licensed, lawful, legitimate, recognized, sanctioned, warranted, and official. Jesus delegated His authority in His name. *HELPS Word Studies* reveals "delegated power refers to the authority God gives to His saints authorizing them to act to the extent they are guided by faith (His revealed word)."

We exercise our authority by faith, not by feelings. The authority to demand the devil loose what belongs to you is yours whether you feel like you've got it or not. You can feel powerless, but the truth is you have the one-two punch of power and authority. Authority has nothing to do with emotions. But you must exercise it for it to be effective.

Jesus has already done everything He's going to do about the devil. He's already done everything He's going to do about sickness. It's up to you to do something now. He is waiting on you to use the authority He gave you to manifest the Kingdom of God in your life.

REVELATION OF AUTHORITY UNLOCKS FAITH TO BATTLE DARKNESS

It's important that you meditate on the authority you have because, like a dog, the enemy can sense when you are walking by fear instead of by faith, doubt instead of belief.

Consider the seven sons of Sceva. Sceva was a Jew and a chief of the priests. As such, his sons were educated in the Word of God. They took it upon themselves to try to cast out evil spirits, saying, "We adjure you by Jesus whom Paul preacheth" (Acts 19:13 KJV).

The only problem was, these seven sons of Sceva didn't have faith in the Word of God made flesh. In other words, they didn't have faith in Jesus and had no basis on which to exercise His authority. They didn't have a relationship with Him. They were not born again. The devils knew they had no authority to use the name. Let's look at the fate of these young men:

> And the evil spirit answered and said, Jesus I know, and Paul I know; but who are ye? And the man in whom the evil spirit was leaped on them, and overcame them, and prevailed against them, so that they fled out of that house naked and wounded (Acts 19:15-16 KJV).

Again, you need a revelation of Christ in you and you in Him to enforce His victory in your life. Jesus said "occupy till I come" (Luke 19:13 KJV). Jesus said to His apostles:

> All authority has been given to Me in heaven and on earth. Go therefore and make disciples of all the nations, baptizing them in the name of the Father and of the Son and of the Holy Spirit, teaching them to observe all things that I have commanded you (Matthew 28:18-20).

He called His twelve disciples to Him and gave them authority over unclean spirits, to cast them out, and to heal all kinds of sickness and all kinds of disease (Matthew 10:1 MEV).

Before His ascension to heaven, Jesus also said:

In My name they will cast out demons; they will speak with new tongues; they will take up serpents; and if they drink anything deadly, it will by no means hurt them; they will lay hands on the sick, and they will recover (Mark 16:17-18).

Jesus expects us to enforce His victory in the earth and has equipped us with every weapon we need—and the authority to use His name. But we need a revelation of authority. Just as our Father in heaven revealed to Peter that Jesus was the Son of the Living God—flesh and blood did not reveal that to him—we need a revelation from heaven. Sitting under teachings about our authority helps open our hearts for God's revelation to pour in, but individual study is imperative.

Jesus is the source of our authority.

Jesus authorizes us. Our authority lies in the name of Jesus. We can't go toe to toe with the devil in our own right.

Therefore God also has highly exalted Him and given Him the name which is above every name, that at the name of Jesus every knee should bow, of those in heaven, and of those on earth, and of those under the earth, and that every tongue should confess that Jesus Christ is Lord, to the glory of God the Father (Philippians 2:9-11).

Jesus authorizes us and empowers us to act in His name. It's His power that backs up our authority. The devil has to bow to the Christ in us when we exercise our authority.

Think about the police officer who is directing traffic. His badge gives him the authority to make you stop. He lifts up his hand and you stop. He doesn't have the physical power in his body to make you stop. You stop because you recognize his authority to make you stop. You know if you don't stop when he says stop, you're illegal and you'll pay a price. The cop exercises his authority in reliance upon the natural government that empowered him. We exercise our authority in reliance on the supernatural government—the kingdom of God—that empowers us.

Our authority is based on what Jesus accomplished. Our authority is not what we accomplish or how well we pray or our feelings or moods. Our authority is not based on our own strength, might, or power. Zechariah 4:6 reveals, "'Not by might nor by power, but by My Spirit,' says the Lord of hosts."

Our faith energizes and activates our authority. Jesus said:

> *These signs will accompany those who believe: In My name they will cast out demons; they will speak with new tongues; they will take up serpents; if they drink any deadly thing, it will not hurt them; they will lay hands on the sick, and they will recover* (Mark 16:17-18 MEV).

God gave us dominion over the earth.

We read about this in Genesis 1:26-28:

Then God said, "Let us make man in our image, after our likeness, and let them have dominion over the fish of the sea, and over the birds of the air, and over the livestock, and over all the earth, and over every creeping thing that creeps on the earth." So God created man in His own image; in the image of God He created him; male and female He created them. God blessed them and said to them, "Be fruitful and multiply, and replenish the earth and subdue it. Rule over the fish of the sea and over the birds of the air and over every living thing that moves on the earth" (MEV).

Psalm 115:16 tells us, "The heavens belong to the Lord, but the earth He has given to the children of men" (MEV).

Adam committed high treason and gave his authority over the earth to satan. The good news is Jesus defeated satan as the Son of Man and took back all authority (see Col. 2:15). He expects us to take authority in the earth and not cede our authority to the wicked one in any area of our lives, families, cities, or nations.

God gives us authority to resist and stand against the devil.

Several scriptures make it clear that this is not only a right, but it's our responsibility as ambassadors for Jesus.

Ephesians 4:27 tells us directly, "Do not give place to the devil" (MEV). The New American Bible (Revised Edition) says "do not leave room for the devil." *The Message* says, "Don't give the Devil that kind of foothold in your life." The Berean Literal Bible says, "Neither give opportunity to the devil." The International Standard Version tells us,

"Do not give the Devil an opportunity to work." The Aramaic Bible in Plain English warns us, "Neither should you give place to The Slanderer." That's pretty clear instruction.

Ephesians 6:13 tells us, "Therefore take up the whole armor of God, that you may be able to withstand in the evil day, and having done all, to stand." The Amplified Bible, Classic Edition makes the point more emphatically: "Therefore put on God's complete armor, that you may be able to resist and stand your ground on the evil day [of danger], and, having done all [the crisis demands], to stand [firmly in your place]." The New Living Translation exhorts us to, "Stand your ground."

James 4:7 tells us, "Therefore submit yourselves to God. Resist the devil, and he will flee from you" (MEV). This goes back to understanding your authority and submitting to authority. If you are not submitted to God's authority, the enemy knows this and has no obligation to flee.

We are seated in heaven in a place of authority.

Ephesians 2:4-7 tells us:

> But God, being rich in mercy, because of His great love with which He loved us, even when we were dead in sins, made us alive together with Christ (by grace you have been saved), and He raised us up and seated us together in the heavenly places in Christ Jesus, so that in the coming ages He might show the surpassing riches of His grace in kindness toward us in Christ Jesus (MEV).

The Spirit that raised Christ from the dead dwells in us.

We're not just seated in heavenly places—far above all principalities and powers—God has also given us incomparably great power (see Eph. 1:19). Indeed, the spirit that raised Christ from the dead dwells in us (see Rom. 8:11). This positions us to have power over all the power of the enemy (see Luke 10:19).

We must actively exercise our authority or it's useless.

Having authority alone is not enough. You can have a bank account full of money and still go hungry if you don't withdraw funds to buy food. The enemy will continue attacking us if we don't exercise our authority. First Peter 5:8-9 tells us, "Be sober and watchful, because your adversary the devil walks around as a roaring lion, seeking whom he may devour. Resist him firmly in the faith, knowing that the same afflictions are experienced by your brotherhood throughout the world" (MEV).

We can't understand our authority with our mind alone. We need to pray for revelation in our spirit.

You can pray this prayer:

Father, in the name of Jesus, I ask You to give me a revelation of the authority Your Son delegated to me. God, open my eyes to the authority that abides in me, in the name of Jesus. Help me understand—to truly understand—the power with which You have endued me so that I can gain the confidence to run to the battle line like David and fight every battle on my path to the destiny you have in store for me, in Jesus' name.

God is waiting for us to take authority in the earth.

Jesus said clearly, "I will give you the keys of the kingdom of heaven, and whatever you bind on earth shall be bound in heaven, and whatever you loose on earth shall be loosed in heaven" (Matt. 16:19 MEV). The New Living Translation puts it this way: "And I will give you the keys of the Kingdom of Heaven. Whatever you forbid on earth will be forbidden in heaven, and whatever you permit on earth will be permitted in heaven."

God's Word Translation says, "I will give you the keys of the kingdom of heaven. Whatever you imprison, God will imprison. And whatever you set free, God will set free." And the Amplified Bible, Classic Edition tells us, "I will give you the keys of the kingdom of heaven; and whatever you bind (declare to be improper and unlawful) on earth must be what is already bound in heaven; and whatever you loose (declare lawful) on earth must be what is already loosed in heaven."

MEDITATE ON YOUR AUTHORITY

Take the time to meditate—really think about—these verses and take any advantage away from the wicked one.

These signs will accompany those who believe: In My name they will cast out demons; they will speak with new tongues; they will take up serpents; if they drink any deadly thing, it will not hurt them; they will lay hands on the sick, and they will recover (Mark 16:17-18 MEV).

I will give you the keys of the kingdom of heaven, and whatever you bind on earth shall be bound in heaven, and whatever you loose on earth shall be loosed in heaven (Matthew 16:19 MEV).

Truly, truly I say to you, he who believes in Me will do the works that I do also. And he will do greater works than these, because I am going to My Father (John 14:12 MEV).

For truly I say to you, whoever says to this mountain, "Be removed and be thrown into the sea," and does not doubt in his heart, but believes that what he says will come to pass, he will have whatever he says (Mark 11:23 MEV).

But you shall receive power when the Holy Spirit comes upon you. And you shall be My witnesses in Jerusalem, and in all Judea and Samaria, and to the ends of the earth (Acts 1:8 MEV).

And they cast out many demons and anointed with oil many who were sick and healed them (Mark 6:13 MEV).

The seventy returned with joy, saying, "Lord, even the demons are subject to us through Your name." He said to them, "I saw Satan as lightning fall from heaven. Look, I give you authority

CLEANSING YOUR HOME FROM EVIL

to trample on serpents and scorpions, and over all the power of the enemy. And nothing shall by any means hurt you" (Luke 10:17-19 MEV).

He called His twelve disciples to Him and gave them authority over unclean spirits, to cast them out, and to heal all kinds of sickness and all kinds of disease (Matthew 10:1 MEV).

You shall tread upon the lion and adder; the young lion and the serpent you shall trample underfoot (Psalm 91:13 MEV).

And to have authority to heal sicknesses and to cast out demons (Mark 3:15 MEV).

Heal the sick, cleanse the lepers, raise the dead, and cast out demons. Freely you have received, freely give (Matthew 10:8 MEV).

CHAPTER 17

KICK THE DEVIL

OUT OF YOUR HOME

Once you are confident of your authority over these demon powers, you can set out to kick the devil out of your home. You can begin to evict them verbally and forcefully in the name of Jesus. Remember, Jesus said:

> *And these signs will follow those who believe: In My name they will cast out demons; they will speak with new tongues; they will take up serpents; and if they drink anything deadly, it will by no means hurt them; they will lay hands on the sick, and they will recover* (Mark 16:17-18).

Jesus has given you authority in your home, and now that you've stripped the enemy of his rights through repentance, he has to go. You need to make a way of escape for the demon powers, so open the doors and windows of your home. Plead the blood of Jesus over your home, and pray this prayer:

> I command every demon power that took up residence in my home to go, now, in Jesus' name. I evict you by the authority of Christ. You have no right to dwell in my home. I put a cease-and-desist order on your foul operations in my midst and command you to go to dry places. You are not welcome in my home. You must go, in Jesus' name.

If you know specific demons that are in your home, such as infirmity or perversion, call them out by name. For example, you would say, "Spirit of _____, I command you to leave my house now, in Jesus' name. I plead the blood of Jesus against you." It's not necessary to know the name of every demon that has taken up residence in your home or that has brought a curse upon you, but if the Lord shows you the name, calling it out can make the fight end more quickly.

The Holy Spirit may also lead you to call on angels for help. Remember this: God commands angels. Humans do not command angels. Psalm 103:20 tells us, "Bless the Lord, you His angels, who are mighty, and do His commands, and obey the voice of His word" (MEV). The New Living Translation of that verse reads: "Praise the Lord, you angels, you mighty ones who carry out his plans, listening for each of his commands." And *The Message* reads, "Bless God, all you armies of angels, alert to respond to whatever he wills. Bless God, all creatures, wherever you are—everything and everyone made by God."

In my book *Angels on Assignment Again*, I offer this prayer on activating warfare angels:

> Father, I thank You that if You are for me, who can be against me? (See Romans 8:31.) I thank You that You are a warrior! You have made me a warrior! You always lead me into triumph in Christ Jesus (see 2 Corinthians 2:14). Thank You for victory in every battle. Thank You for wisdom, strategies, and insight from the Holy Spirit. Thank You for my supernatural weapons. And I thank You for Your warring angels. I ask You to dispatch them now, on my behalf, in Jesus' name!

You need to continue pleading the blood of Jesus and commanding demons to flee until you feel a breakthrough in your spirit. The Bible speaks of warfare as a wrestling match, and sometimes you have to wrestle the demons because stubborn devils that have been living in your home will typically not leave without some resistance. You'll have to stand your ground like you would with a flesh and blood thief in your home.

CHAPTER 18

SHUTTING
THE DEVIL OUT FOR GOOD

Didn't that feel good? Now that you cleansed your home from evil—now that you kicked the devil out of your house—you need to shut the door for good. Keep this in mind: It's not enough to slam the door in the devil's face. He won't stop with a little rejection. He's persistent. Knowing this, be vigilant to padlock your premises after the forced eviction. You need to stay on the offense and be the steward God has called you to be, deciding what comes in and out of your home with due diligence.

Put another way, you are gatekeeper of your home. Part of shutting the devil out of your home is understanding your role as the gatekeeper. A gatekeeper is one who controls access to a place. In this case, that place is your home. The gatekeeper's job is to forbid demonic intruders no matter how they masquerade themselves. By this point, you have learned all too well that satan disguises himself as an angel of light (see 2 Cor. 11:14).

Put another way, the enemy often comes in through a Trojan horse. You may remember the story from the Trojan War, during which the Greek army built a magnificent, giant wooden horse and left it outside the gate of the city of Troy. The gatekeepers of Troy were fascinated and pulled the wooden structure inside the city, never suspecting the Greek army was inside waiting for an opportune time to strike. Ultimately, the Greeks destroyed the city of Troy in an embarrassing defeat.

The devil used the Trojan horse strategy long before the Greeks existed. Indeed, this wile of the enemy dates back to the Book of Beginnings. In Genesis 3, we read how satan came into the Garden of Eden through what looked like an innocent snake. Remember, God brought all the animals before Adam to see what he would name them, so Adam was the one who named the snake a snake. But Eve didn't discern satan was hiding inside the creature and using the snake God created to deliver a message that would lead to the fall of man and a curse on the ground.

In modern days, computer hackers use Trojan horses to inject viruses into your computer. When a virus strikes your computer, it's akin to it having a proverbial curse upon it. The computer may run slowly until you notice the curse. Sometimes the virus even takes over the entire machine or renders it disabled until you pay a ransom. Thank God, He is our Redeemer.

Now back to the Garden. Adam was a gatekeeper in the Garden of Eden. Eve had her part to play as his helpmate, but she did not discern the ways of God and was deceived by the snake's tempting words. Adam was the fail-safe, but he, too, fell to the enemy's deception. Yes, it can happen to anyone—and it does. In order to discern what God wants in or out of your house and to avoid falling for the temptation of the Trojan horse, you as a gatekeeper must understand the laws of the Kingdom.

Throughout the pages of this book, your eyes have been opened to the devices of the devil. You are no longer uninformed about accursed objects and other avenues through which demon powers are allowed to enter freely, dwell securely, and wreak havoc on your life. Armed with this information, you have an upper hand on these tyrannical trespassers. But be warned, the devil will try to get back in. Your house has been delivered from evil.

SEVEN TIMES WORSE?

Speaking of deliverance, Jesus once said:

When an unclean spirit goes out of a man, he goes through dry places, seeking rest, and finds none. Then he says, "I will return to my house from which I came." And when he comes, he finds it empty, swept, and put in order. Then he goes and takes with him seven other spirits more wicked than himself, and they enter and dwell there; and the last state of that man is worse than the first (Matthew 12:43-45).

Let's look at *The Message* version of this passage for good measure:

When a defiling evil spirit is expelled from someone, it drifts along through the desert looking for an oasis, some unsuspecting soul it can bedevil. When it doesn't find anyone, it says,

"I'll go back to my old haunt." On return it finds the person spotlessly clean, but vacant. It then runs out and rounds up seven other spirits more evil than itself and they all move in, whooping it up. That person ends up far worse off than if he'd never gotten cleaned up in the first place.

You might say, "Well, that's talking about people not homes." Be assured, the same principle applies. *Elliot's Commentary for English Readers* offers a sobering thought: "The number seven, as in the case of Mary Magdalene, represents a greater intensity of possession, showing itself in more violent paroxysms of frenzy, and with less hope of restoration." Of course, with God there is always hope of restoration. But that's not the point. If you let these demons back in through carelessness or apathy, it may be hard to get them out the next time. Don't do it!

While these commentaries apply to casting demons out of humans, you can expect the same reactions from demons when they go out of your home. If they don't find another home to occupy, they will try to get back into yours. Shutting the devil out for good, then, means more than merely staying on guard against objects, media, and other means through which the enemy can terrorize your life. After you empty, do a clean sweep, and put your house back in order, you need to fill it with God's presence.

In John 14:23, Jesus said, "If anyone loves Me, he will keep My word; and My Father will love him, and We will come to him and make Our home with him." The Amplified Bible, Classic Edition reads, "Jesus answered, If a person [really] loves Me, he will keep My word [obey My teaching]; and My Father will love him, and We will come to him and make Our home (abode, special dwelling place) with him." Although this was talking about being one with God in our spirits, it is equally true of our physical homes.

BLESS YOUR HOME

Since there were accursed objects in your home, the first step to eradicating demons once and for all is replacing the curse with a blessing. You want God's blessing on your home. When you decide, as Joshua did, that you and your house will serve the Lord (see Josh. 24:15), you can confidently ask for God's blessing on your home. This is part of the covenant.

Proverbs 3:33 tells us, "The curse of the Lord is on the house of the wicked, but He blesses the home of the just." Deuteronomy promises when we obey the Lord we will be blessed coming in and blessed going out (see Deut. 28:6). And Proverbs 3:24 says, "When you lie down, you will not be afraid; yes, you will lie down and your sleep will be sweet." Pray this prayer:

> Father, in the name of Jesus, we choose to serve You with our whole heart. We choose to hate evil and love what is good. Bless our home with protection, unity, and joy. Let Your peace dwell here. Bless us with discernment to avoid letting the enemy back into our home.

DEDICATE YOUR HOME TO THE LORD

Start by dedicating or rededicating your home to the Lord. I live in South Florida where there is a heavy Jewish population. When I purchased my first condo, it had a mezuzah on the door frame. The practice comes from Deuteronomy 6:6-9:

> *And these words which I command you today shall be in your heart. You shall teach them diligently to your children, and shall talk of them when you sit in your house, when you walk by the way, when you lie down, and when you rise up. You shall bind them as a sign on your hand, and they shall be as frontlets between your eyes. You shall write them on the doorposts of your house and on your gates.*

Hung on an angle of the doorpost, the mezuzah contains parchment paper with words from the Torah and marks the house as belonging to one who is in covenant with God. It's a symbol that tells the enemy the house belongs to Jehovah. That is one way of dedicating your house to God in terms of a prophetic act, but we have to go deeper if we want to drive the devil out for good.

Of course, you don't need a mezuzah. You can dedicate your home to the Lord in prayer. Pray this prayer: "Father, in the name of Jesus, we invite You to dwell here. We dedicate our home for You and Your use. We say You are the Lord of our home. All that we have is Yours."

After Solomon built and dedicated the temple, the Lord said, "Now My eyes will be open and My ears attentive to prayer made in this place. For now I have chosen and sanctified this house, that My name may be there forever; and My eyes and My heart will be there perpetually" (2 Chron. 7:15-16). This is the power of dedicating your home to the Lord and meaning it.

Anoint the Thresholds

Anoint all thresholds—gates into your home—with oil. This doesn't have to be overcomplicated. If you don't have official anointing oil, you can get some olive oil and ask your pastor to bless it. Or you can bless it yourself. Oil is a symbol of the Holy Spirit.

The practice of anointing your thresholds is biblical: "And you shall take the anointing oil, and anoint the tabernacle and all that is in it; and you shall hallow it and all its utensils, and it shall be holy" (Exod. 40:9). We anoint the thresholds, including doors and windows, as protection at the gates of our home.

Build a Family Altar

A family altar is a place for devotions. If you live alone, you can still build an altar to the Lord in your home. This should be a quiet place, not in front of the TV but perhaps in a room that is less used for other activities. I have a prayer chair. It's an area where I study and pray. Pray often. The enemy hates the sound of your prayers.

Continue in Praise and Worship

Keep praise and worship music on in your home—even when you are not there. It may not be practical to have worship music playing the whole time you are home due to other activities in which you must engage. But when you are not home, there's nothing stopping you from letting worship music play continuously.

The Bible says we enter His courts with praise (see Ps. 100:4). The Bible says in His presence there is fullness of joy (see Ps. 16:11). The Bible says the joy of the Lord is our strength (see Neh. 8:10). See, the enemy knows if you can get in the presence of God through praise, you can find peace for your soul, joy in your spirit, and strength to battle back against his schemes. The enemy hates hearing it. The same holds true for worship.

Play the Word of God

You can also leave a CD or YouTube audio of the Word of God playing in your home continually. Hebrews 4:12 assures, "For the word of God is living and powerful, and sharper than any two-edged sword, piercing even to the division of soul and spirit, and of joints and marrow, and is a discerner of the thoughts and intents of the heart."

And in Ephesians 6:17, Paul exhorts us to take up the sword of the Spirit, which is the Word of God. Paul wasn't necessarily admonishing you to carry it around as a fashion statement like a cross on a necklace or a T-shirt with a Bible verse. Paul meant to be prepared to wield that Spirit in the heat of the good fight of faith. Let the Word emanate through your house and demons will not want to stick around.

In fact, if you want to get Kingdom violent about it, leave the worship music playing in one room and the Word playing in another and a preacher on Christian TV in another!

Maintain an Atmosphere of Love and Peace

When you cultivate an atmosphere of love in your home, God will feel welcomed there. By contrast, God hates strife. God is love, and where love is expressed God dwells. Ephesians 5:2 tells us to walk in love.

When you do these things, the glory of the Lord will fill your home. After Solomon built the temple, they didn't leave it empty. They immediately brought the ark of the covenant—which carries the presence of God—into the temple. What happened next is astounding: "And it came to pass, when the priests came out of the holy place, that the cloud filled the house of the Lord, so that the priests could not continue ministering because of the cloud; for the glory of the Lord filled the house of the Lord" (1 Kings 8:10-11).

When your home is fully dedicated to the Lord and you make Him feel welcome there, it will repel the enemy. Yes, you can still defile your home in the future, but the enemy is much less likely to want to hang out in a home that is full of the glory just the same way thieves are less likely to break into a home in which all the lights are on. When the light of the Lord shines in your home, it repels demon powers.

Prayer Walk Around Your Home

Finally, prayer walk through and around your home. Pray in the spirit or just walk through the home praising the Lord and thanking Him for His protection and blessing. Ask God to surround your house with favor like a shield (see Ps. 5:12).

FINAL WORDS OF ADVICE

If you should in the future find something someone brought in your home that resembles a cursed object, swiftly follow the process to destroy it and pray to cleanse your home. If you later find that you've unknowingly brought something in your home that grieves the Lord or find something you previously missed, engage in the practices found in this book and all will be well.

Don't walk in paranoia. If you are flipping the channels on your television and something unseemly pops up, the enemy isn't going to come back in like a flood during those three seconds. So long as you don't invite the enemy in through objects or agree with the enemy in your heart—and as long as you create an atmosphere where the Lord feels at home—you and your house will walk in freedom. Angels will encamp around you and your home because of your reverential fear of the Lord (see Ps. 34:7).

ABOUT
JENNIFER LECLAIRE

Jennifer LeClaire is senior leader of Awakening House of Prayer in Fort Lauderdale, Florida, founder of the Ignite Network, and founder of the Awakening Prayer Hubs prayer movement. Jennifer served as the first-ever female editor of *Charisma* magazine and is a prolific author of over 50 books. You can find Jennifer online or shoot her an email at info@jenniferleclaire.org.